OTHER BOOKS BY SARAH YORK

Pilgrim Heart: The Inner Journey Home

Remembering Well: Rituals for Celebrating Life and Mourning Death

Into the Wilderness

THE HOLY INTIMACY OF STRANGERS

JOSSEY-BASS
A Wiley Imprint
www.josseybass.com

Published by Jossey-Bass
A Wiley Imprint
989 Market Street, San Francisco, CA 94103-1741   www.josseybass.com

Bible quotations, unless otherwise noted, are from *The New Oxford Annotated Bible with Apocrypha*, edited by Herbert G. May and Bruce M. Metzger. New York: Oxford University Press, 1977.

Jossey-Bass books and products are available through most bookstores. To contact Jossey-Bass directly call our Customer Care Department within the U.S. at 800-956-7739, outside the U.S. at 317-572-3986 or fax 317-572-4002.

Jossey-Bass also publishes its books in a variety of electronic formats. Some content that appears in print may not be available in electronic books.

Library of Congress Cataloging-in-Publication Data

York, Sarah, date-
  The holy intimacy of strangers / Sarah York.— 1st ed.
      p. cm.
Includes bibliographical references.
  ISBN 0-7879-6047-0 (alk. paper)
  1. Strangers—Religious aspects. 2. Intimacy (Psychology)—Religious aspects. 3. Interpersonal relations—Religious aspects. I. Title.

BL626.33 .Y67 2002
241'.671—dc21   2002005439

Printed in the United States of America
FIRST EDITION
HB Printing 10 9 8 7 6 5 4 3 2 1

CONTENTS

For Jerry
and in memory of strangers
who died in terrorist attacks on the United States
September 11, 2001

A NOTE TO READERS

This is a book about getting past fear of the stranger, about living in community with other human beings, about feeling part of the holy scheme of life. It is a book about trust, and how vital it is that we be able to trust people in all kinds of relationship.

Trust, however, took a major hit on September 11, 2001, when members of Islamic radical terrorist networks organized by Osama bin Laden hijacked four large commercial airplanes and flew them on a mission of hate. Their collisions with the twin towers of the World Trade Center and the Pentagon, along with the crashing of the fourth plane in Pennsylvania, resulted in the tragic deaths of more than three thousand people.

Half of this book was written before September 11. I realized immediately after the attacks that the themes I had chosen were, in fact, themes for reflecting on the tragic events of that day. I was unable to write a word for two weeks after September 11, but when I resumed writing, it was with a deeper sense of how important it is that we call ourselves into holy space with strangers and build relationships of trust and solidarity.

I have dedicated this book to a close personal friend. In keeping with the themes of intimacy and strangeness, I have also dedicated it to the memory of the strangers who died on September 11 as a result of the terrorist attack. May this book honor them, as it invites us all to work toward trust and goodwill among strangers everywhere.

GRATITUDES

The Holy Intimacy of Strangers was conceived in England, where I lived for six months while serving as minister to the Rosslyn Hill Unitarian Chapel in London. Since my husband had his work in the United States, I lived alone most of the time, "a stranger in a strange land." There, as a foreigner who had much to learn about the British people and their culture, I was forced daily to depend on strangers, who suffered my cultural blunders and helped me venture beyond my own secure territory. To the gracious people in London—particularly the strangers at Rosslyn Hill Chapel who became my friends—I am grateful, for supporting me through lonely or fearful times, and for reminding me of how precious the connections are that we make with the human family.

With this, my third book for Jossey-Bass/Wiley, I have grown in appreciation for the terrific team of people who help me improve my writing without intruding on the creative process, particularly Sheryl Fullerton, my editor, who shared the vision for this volume from the beginning and shepherded it along with personal sensitivity and spiritual insight. Sheryl and Mark Kerr, marketing manager, lead the wonderful folks of the Jossey-Bass Religion in Practice team through the process of getting ideas and stories into print and circulation. It has been a privilege and a joy, once again, to work with Sheryl and Mark, as well as Joanne Clapp Fullagar, Chandrika Madhavan, Jessica Egbert, and Thomas Finnegan, all of whom participate in a sense of their publishing mission, exhibit pride in their work, and function well as a team. Barbara Moulton helped get this book launched; I have really enjoyed working with her.

I am deeply grateful to my readers: Lee Blue, Jerry Godard, Janet Harvey, Jere Jacob, and Ann Lewis. They are friends who challenge and affirm my work in the spirit of love, and every chapter has benefited from their wise counsel. My husband, Chuck, has been my chief source of support. Knowing my professional pitfalls better than anyone, he helps me keep perspective and has been the first to offer honest feedback to each chapter.

Without the richness of examples from diverse perspectives, this book could not have been written; I want to thank all those who contributed their personal stories. I was blessed with more wonderful anecdotes than I could include. In a few instances, I have used composite examples or changed some details to protect the privacy of people who preferred to be anonymous.

Finally, I offer my deep gratitude to the strangers, named and unnamed, who have enriched my life and inspired me to write this book.

June 2002

Sarah York
Asheville, North Carolina

THE HOLY
INTIMACY
OF STRANGERS

INTRODUCTION

On a warm southern afternoon in early April, two-year-old Caleb's grandfather, Poppa, organized a picnic in the city park. Poppa, a friend of mine, told me about something wonderful that happened that day.

While Caleb's parents finished their meal, he and Poppa headed toward the pond, where a teenager was helping a three-year-old feed the ducks. The teenager had left his guitar leaning against a bench. Caleb, obsessed by musical instruments, raced to grab the guitar and was scooped up by his mother, Renee, who quickly apologized. Poppa sought to bridge the awkwardness of the encounter and spoke with the young man, whose name was Shawn, about the early attraction to music evinced by some young children. He learned that Shawn himself was such a child, schooled on the violin, then saxophone and keyboard, before teaching himself the guitar. Shawn was not yet seventeen. The child feeding the ducks was his daughter, Tiara.

At Poppa's request, Shawn played his guitar for the whole family, but Caleb and Tiara grew restless, so Renee walked back to the pond with them. Tiara shared a bag of Bunny Bread with Caleb, and the two of them fed the ducks with delight until an aggressive goose startled Caleb. Tiara, not much bigger than Caleb or the goose, stepped bravely between them, saying, "You goose, get out of my brother's face!"

When Renee and the children returned to the others, Poppa was trying to sing harmony with Shawn. Caleb stopped, and stood entranced in front of Shawn, watching him play the guitar for about ten minutes. Then, ever so carefully, Caleb touched, and then strummed, the guitar's strings in perfect rhythm while Shawn fingered the chords.

By nightfall, these strangers, from different racial and cultural backgrounds, had become a family group. In silent recognition of their bond, and with moist eyes all around, they embraced, each with every other, in dawning awareness of the grace that had blessed their time together.

"You goose, get out of my brother's face!" Tiara's command rolled naturally from her tongue, as she stepped in to defend Caleb. This description of families who became family—or, more accurately, who recognized that they *were* family—captures and fills my heart with its grace, its promise, and its testimony to the sacred bond that exists among all human beings.

Encounters such as this inspired me to write about the holy intimacy of strangers. When I tested the proposed title for this book on friends and acquaintances, it was typical to see them become animated with inner resonance. "Oh, yes," they might say, "I know what you mean. I recall one time when I was on a flight to South Africa. . . ."

Parks, airplanes, and grocery stores; city streets and country lanes; museums and shopping malls; trains and elevators—these are a few of the settings for our daily interaction with strangers. Most of the time, these encounters are not what we would describe either as holy or intimate. Occasionally, however, we feel the power of grace breaking in on an experience with a stranger and exposing the walls of insulation or estrangement that divide us from others. Our recognition of a transcendent linkage in our interaction breaches the barriers that separate us from our sense of belonging in the human family.

As the world shrinks and we grow more conscious of ourselves as citizens of a global village, our need for the experience of human bonding expands. Yet we tend to create tribal associations that bring us into contact with people who are like us rather than different from us. Longing for community, we are drawn to a church, club, or association, but our experience can become more a retreat from the world than engagement with it. Anne Morrow Lindbergh captures a sense of our ambivalence while she expresses the personally enriching aspect of reaching beyond our tighter circle of relationship when we choose those with whom we want to associate: "[We] tend to select people like ourselves, a very monotonous diet. All hors d'oeuvres and no meat; or all sweets and no vegetables, depending on the kind of people we are. But . . . one thing is fairly certain: we usually select the known, seldom the strange. We tend not to choose the unknown which might be a shock or a disappointment or simply a little difficult to cope with. And yet it is the unknown with all its disappointments and surprises that is the most enriching."[1]

It is to some of our extraordinary experiences with strangers, then, that we can look for a taste of the kind of association that satisfies our deep hunger for intimacy, not only with strangers but also with the stranger inside each one of us. Our encounters with strangers, when viewed with an eye toward nourishing human community, invite us into a deeper, more committed relationship with the Spirit.[2]

The Spirit reveals itself to us in our relationship with our world and its inhabitants; it is the source of all that is holy, sacred, and true. The word *spirit* comes from the Latin word meaning "breath"; the word *holy* derives from before the Christian era from words for whole as well as health, good luck, and happiness. The *holy* intimacy of strangers, then, is an experience of the Spirit's promise and power, breathed into human interaction and calling us into personal and spiritual wholeness—into the kind of harmony that yields health and happiness.

The notion of intimacy with strangers poses an intriguing paradox: we encounter the familiar in the unfamiliar, the known in the unknown, the self in the other, and the other in the self. The word *intimacy* appeared in the seventeenth century in English, from Latin by way of sixteenth-century French, deriving from words for inner or inmost. Intimacy in relationship refers to the deepest, closest, and most profound associations. The word *stranger,* deriving from the Old French word *estrange,* evokes the opposite in its meaning, as it points to what is "external, foreign, outside, or without." To speak of intimacy with strangers is to experience a deep and profound closeness or innerness with what is most foreign or external to us.

In Hebrew, the word for stranger is *zar,* which means "border." This meaning adds another dimension to our thinking about how we relate with strangers. An invitation into intimate connection with the stranger is a beckoning from across some of the boundaries, barriers, or estrangements that separate us.

Crossing the boundary of our own consciousness into that of the stranger gives us a perspective we do not normally have. As we move through some of the barriers that divide us—our fears and our prejudices, mostly—we discover that the stranger is not so very strange after all. The stranger, writes Marilyn Sewell, is really just someone else like you or me: "We are not separate; we are one. No strangers, really, just part of our lost selves reclaimed."[3]

An encounter with a stranger is like a mirror held up to our own true nature. We learn who we are by observing how we respond to a stranger. Isn't it curious, for example, that we are sometimes inclined to reveal our innermost secrets to a total stranger while seated on an airplane, but we will not be so open with our best friends? Why is it that we sometimes let loose with angry expletives for another driver in traffic but cannot seem to express a resentment to someone in our own family?

In our interactions with strangers, we recognize, reclaim, and even learn to love our lost selves. Then (coming full circle into a "whole" relationship), as we become better acquainted with the stranger inside us, we also become more hospitable to the strangers among us.

When I set out to write this book, I designed it so that each chapter could be read apart from the rest, and in any order the reader might choose. Although I think you can read any chapter alone without feeling confused, I found myself introducing themes in the first several chapters that are developed more deeply in the final chapters. There is, then, a subtle progression of themes, at the same time that each chapter stands on its own.

As a minister, I have always preached to myself first. As a writer, I write to explore my own spiritual growing edges. This book has surely taken me there, to those edges, where I struggle with my demons of fear, my shadows of cowardice, or my need to tidy up the messy business of life.

As I invite you, the reader, into the chapters of this book, I invite you also to enter into a dialogue with yourself and others, a conversation that will take you into your own memories of grace-tinged encounters as well as your fears of strangeness. May you also venture into the public arena, where your encounters with strangers deepen your connection with your inner voice of truth, with your human companions, and with the Spirit.

*To speak of intimacy with strangers is
to experience a deep and profound
closeness or innerness with what is
most foreign or external to us.*

CHAPTER ONE

MOMENT OF TRUTH

ONE SUNDAY MORNING AFTER A CHURCH SERVICE, I was meeting with members of my congregation when someone came and whispered to me that there was a strange man waiting in the vestibule. He wanted to see the minister. I knew what that meant: he wanted money, of course, and what better time to be sure to catch the minister at church than on a Sunday morning?

I left the meeting. As I approached the man, I could smell the alcohol on his breath immediately when he spoke. He said, "I want to pray and to turn my life over to Jesus."

Sure you do, I thought, feeling less than charitable and wishing I was anyone but the minister at that moment. I explained that the congregation was gathering for a meeting and suggested that he might find someone available at another church down the street. "No," he said.

"That doesn't matter. I just need to be able to pray right now. I have really messed up my life with drugs and alcohol, and I want to make a new start. All I need is a place to pray."

"Well," I said, still expecting to be asked for money, "as you can see, there is a meeting going on in the church. There really isn't an appropriate place for—"

"That doesn't matter," he interrupted. "I just need to pray, *now*. This is my moment of truth. *Now*. It has to be *now*." Then he repeated, "This is my moment of truth."

"I suppose we could go into my office," I said, still thinking that the church down the street would be better able to serve this man's need.

As we entered my office, he fell immediately to his knees and amid sobs he began praying. About that time, I finally caught on. He really had come to church to pray! As he prayed, I placed my hands on his shoulders; when he was finished, I asked him his name and offered a prayer, too, saying his name and asking God to forgive him and give him the strength to change and make amends to his family. Then I talked with him for a few minutes about support groups and drug programs. He left, and I went back to the meeting.

His moment of truth? Yes. But it was my moment of truth, too, because in those few moments when that man was on his knees, I let go of my fear; I let go of my distrust; I let go of my judging. I let go of my awareness of the tremendous gap between what he believed and what I believed. It was, indeed, a moment of truth. It was a moment of holy intimacy, where we two strangers each encountered our own fears and flaws and were held in a bond of sacred trust.

I have shared many precious moments with people in counseling or in conversation, and there has often been an element of grace in those times because of a spiritual connection between us. But in this moment of truth, there was a power at work that brought this strange man and me into a common territory, a territory where human souls connect with each other in a sacred dimension.

In that sacred space, I was not only moved by the power of the moment but given an opportunity to reflect on my own moment of truth, for I had to contend with fears that were uncomfortable for me. For one thing, I was afraid of my own inadequacy. I was the minister of a liberal (Unitarian Universalist) church where we were not accustomed to speaking in terms of "turning our lives over to Jesus." This man was asking for something that was not part of my usual repertoire of pastoral or liturgical offerings. I squirmed within the narrow confines of my own religious perspective, awkward and unwilling to venture into the holy space where I might have to compromise how I express my religious beliefs in order to be present with the stranger.

I was also afraid of being made to feel foolish. So my defenses were in place. If, as I suspected, the stranger wanted money to support his drug habit rather than prayer to help him kick it, I was determined to be wise to his deceptive attempt to weaken my resolve with his story about wanting to pray. I did not want him to take advantage of my goodwill.

But the fear beneath each of these feelings was something more disturbing. My real moment of truth came when I realized that I was not in charge of the situation. When I would hear stories from strangers about why they wanted money, I often chose to believe them and could help them without giving them cash. I gave them restaurant or bus vouchers, or I wrote a check to the phone company from a special discretionary account. I made referrals to other agencies. There was generally something I could do. When this stranger asked for holy presence, however, I could not open a drawer and salve my conscience or hasten his exit with a simple gesture of charity.

My moment of truth was the recognition of a boundary that had, as a result of my own defensive posture, inhibited my receptiveness to spiritual power and my ability to help a person in need. The Spirit blessed this encounter, not *because* of me, but in spite of me.

Reflecting on my cautious skepticism, I have had to ask, "Suppose this man was just making up the story about wanting to change just to soften me up. What would I lose by believing him? So what, if I'm a fool? What do I lose? Nothing—except control. And so what if the moment evokes an emotional response—a man whose name I don't even know, kneeling and praying and sobbing in my presence? What is there to fear? Nothing—except loss of control. And suppose I am moved to tears myself. What am I afraid of? Nothing—except not having control."

So that is what the real moment of truth was about. I think the moment of truth comes for most of us when we come up against something we cannot control. For me, it meant confronting my awkwardness, my discomfort, my fears, and my resistance. It meant examining my own understanding of God, too. I may as well have said to the man, "I'm sorry, but your God really doesn't live in this church, and my deity is an all-encompassing principle that has neither gender nor ears." The irony is that my expansive god-force would turn out to be smaller than his father in heaven. In the moment of truth that was a moment of grace, it didn't matter. It just did not matter.

What *does* matter? The moment of truth is a moment of connection, that's all—with the unnamable Spirit, with ourselves, with other human beings who are willing to admit (or perhaps even invite) loss of control. In this surrender to holy possibility and this openness to a common human experience that transcends our particular perspectives, we meet the deep core of ourselves that is not defined by systems of belief, and not threatened by another point of view or a different way of being. This does not mean we lose our individual selves or change what we think; it just means we meet at a level where, having surrendered a layer of identity to a divine or transcendent purpose, we participate in a holy intimacy and receive power from the connection.

STRANGERS AT HOME

A grace-filled connection that occurs with a stranger stirs reflection about how we also defend ourselves against intimacy in our more familiar relationships. Sometimes it is easier to be open to significant connection with a stranger than with our most intimate companions. The issues that we have to confront are the same, however: fear of inadequacy, pride, or stubbornness; hesitation about a situation where someone might take advantage of us; a need to feel we have some control. Although we long to make deep personal and spiritual connection with those we love, we may sometimes find ourselves feeling as though they are strangers to us. We may live according to habitual patterns, or take each other's presence for granted. In simply enjoying one another's companionship, we may not be inclined to explore deeper ways of being together. Perhaps we create ways to avoid conflict or an uncomfortable topic of conversation.

Our moments of truth often occur with family and friends, just as they do with strangers, when we meet a life crisis. Not only do we increase our consciousness of how precious our time is together; we are more aware of our powerlessness and our need for one another when we experience a decline in health, or lose a job, or go through a divorce, or face death, or face the death of someone we love.

One such moment of truth occurred for me in the four days I spent with my father before he died. We had always enjoyed a very loving relationship and never lacked for things to talk about, but our conversation had rarely gone deeper than speculation about whether it would rain, or admiration of a good double play executed by the White Sox. But during our last four days together, I made some precious connections with him, and with my older brother, the only other surviving member of my family of origin.

As my father's kidneys began to fail, I asked the doctor if there was anything he could do. I will not forget his words. "There's always something we can do," he said, allowing his sentence to sit on the air between us, unpunctuated. I completed his train of thought in my mind. Yes, there is always something we *can* do, but *should* we? It became apparent that any measures taken by the medical team would only prolong my father's illness and require that he remain in the hospital for an extended time. I asked the doctor to inform him of the situation and of his options. Knowing how much my father dreaded suffering through a long terminal illness, I knew he would not choose to go on dialysis.

I went into his hospital room after the conference with the doctor. "I guess you just got some bad news," I said. "No," said my father, smiling, "good news." His worst fear had been assuaged. "I understand," I said, and then I lay on his bed beside him and sobbed. He understood too.

For several hours, we were present with each other as never before. As a cartoonist who had only a day earlier been honored with the National Cartoonist Society award for Best Story Strip ("Gasoline Alley"), he grieved for the stories he would not write. "I have lots more stories in me," he said, relieved that he would not have to plot the demise of Walt Wallet, the aging patriarch of his comic strip, during his lifetime. He shared some of his personal regrets, but he was not afraid of dying. "I have had a good life," he said, with gratitude. He told me where to find important documents and explained provisions in his will. I had never been able to ask him about such matters, since to do so would have been to introduce the topic of his eventual death—not something I wanted to bring up.

Knowing that death was imminent, I called my brother, who is a heart surgeon. "Come here *now*," I told him. But he could not accept this sense of urgency. He wanted every medical alternative explored, including dialysis. We argued for several minutes, and then finally I screamed at him, "Daddy is dying! Get on a plane as soon as you can and get yourself out here, damn it!"

My brother arrived the next evening. A few hours after my brother visited with him, our father died. Since then, I have been closer with my brother—able to talk about personal issues that we previously avoided. The moment of truth that surfaced our fear, anger, and despair when our father died was also the moment of grace that invited the presence of the holy into our midst. In the fifteen years since that time, we have related to one another at an intimate level. Although we have our regrets with regard to unexplored depths in our relationship with other family members, we strive to maintain honest communication, which requires that we continue to let go of the fears and defenses that create a barrier to our bond of love and trust.

It does not have to be a loss or tragedy that opens you to the moment of truth. It might be anything that brings you to your knees—literally or figuratively. The moment of truth is a moment of humility and perspective on the self. It might occur when you look out at the stars on a clear night in the desert and get a little perspective on what you do and do not control. Or you may witness the birth of a child and experience the power of creation that is not of your making. These are times when we are brought to our knees—when we are invited to let go of our illusion of power and participate in the creative power of it all. Whether we are humbled by our own inadequacy, touched by the overwhelming beauty of creation, or confronted with the mystery of death, we are acutely aware of how little control we really have. Choices, yes—we have choices about how we will respond to the events of our lives. But when we fool ourselves into thinking we can control those events, we construct an inner barrier that prevents us from experiencing the spiritual power that is available to us.

LOSING CONTROL, GAINING POWER

In the moments of truth I have experienced, I discovered something important: by letting go of my need to be in charge of the situation and allowing myself to be vulnerable, I confronted my own fears. As I met the fears and let go of them, they had less power. In a way, I gained control by being willing to lose it.

If we can receive power by being willing to face what we do not control, we can also *lose* power by *not* being willing to face what we cannot control. What it boils down to is that if we have a strong need for control, we are much more likely to become anxious when we don't have it. The higher our level of anxiety, the more likely we are to become stressed or depressed. In fact, the higher our level of anxiety, the more vulnerable we are to any number of health problems. The cycle escalates; more need for control means more anxiety, and more anxiety means more symptoms.

I recall speaking with a friend who remarked, "I feel like my life is living me instead of me living my life." This was more than a yearning for a life that was less busy or less stressful. He was saying that he did not make choices in his life, that he just reacted to what happened to him.

The paradox of trying to gain control of a life that is out of control is that it is likely to spin ever more out of control. Joseph Campbell, with his gift for distilling the wisdom of the world's religions into archetypal images that speak the language of the soul, spoke of living out of the hub of the wheel instead of the rim. That is the difference between living your life instead of being lived by it. Writer Ann Morrow Lindbergh described what that might feel like: "I want a singleness of eye, a purity of intention, a central core to my life that will enable me to carry out [my] obligations and activities as well as I can. I want . . . to live 'in grace' as much of the time as possible. By grace I mean an inner harmony, essentially spiritual, which can be translated into an outward harmony."[1]

Call it the spiritual core. Call it the hub. Call it the inner light. Call it the spiritual center of the self, which lives life instead of being lived by it. It is this aspect of soul that gives us our meaning and purpose because it aligns us with spiritual purpose.

When my friend confessed that he felt his life was living him, it was a moment of truth for him. He also admitted that he was drinking heavily, but he said he found it humiliating to consider going to Alcoholics Anonymous. I told him that it was humbling—it was humility, not humiliation. Humiliation derives from self-centeredness and pride. Humility is self-centering, that is, it centers the individual in the Spirit and in a larger purpose. Humiliation is what he would suffer if he did not do something to regain his inner freedom. Humility, on the other hand, was the Spirit's way of nudging him toward health, and toward the kind of inner spiritual grace that would enable him to give as he was meant to give.

People who have participated in twelve-step programs designed to assist them with the problems of addiction understand the importance of recognizing their powerlessness. For them, the moment of truth is when they "hit bottom"—when they admit they do not have the power to overcome their addiction. Like the stranger who came to me that Sunday morning wanting to turn his life over to Jesus, many come to their first twelve-step meeting ready to "turn their life over" to a higher power. To admit their powerlessness is an act of courage, for it is stepping into unknown territory. It is painfully humbling. But twelve-step programs work, and one reason they work is because "anonymous" strangers help one another recognize their powerlessness and call upon a power higher than their own.

Letting go of the illusion of control means shedding some of the insulation that protects us from receiving the gifts of life. Consider the effects of any addiction, whether it is to food or alcohol or drugs, or gambling, or sex, or shopping, or surfing the Internet. Saint Augustine is reported to have said that God is always trying to give good things to us, but our hands are too full to receive them. Addiction keeps our hands full. It is any compulsive, habitual behavior that limits one's freedom to make choices. Some addictions are more destructive than others, but any addiction robs you of your inner freedom and is therefore damaging to your spirit. You become a slave to whatever appetite demands that it be satisfied. Addiction disrupts the natural balance that your body, mind, and spirit seek to achieve, so that you may live in grace, or out of the hub.

The process of turning your life over to God or Spirit, or a higher power of your own definition, is a process of reclaiming your life and your freedom. The paradox is that by acknowledging your powerlessness over the addiction, you receive strength and power. By forgetting yourself and acknowledging your lack of control, you gain freedom and direction for your life. It is, to use the language of Jesus, the process of losing your life in order to gain it.

GIFTS FROM STRANGERS

The moment of truth becomes the moment when we become aware of what it is that keeps our hands (and lives) too full to receive the gifts of life. It is often in the company of strangers that we are invited to empty our hands and our lives and open ourselves to the gifts of grace and the guidance of the Spirit.

Such was the case for the young man who interrupted Betsy Bunn and some of her fellow members of Emmanuel Church in the City of

Boston, as they gathered in Lindsey Chapel after a fire had gutted their sanctuary. It was a few weeks before Christmas, and bitter cold. The people who gathered for evening prayer felt more than ever a sense of gratitude for the warmth and safety of their space, poignantly aware that warmth and safety can be fragile.

The stranger's appearance caught the group off guard. Bunn writes:

After the prayer service a small group gathered to talk about the coming holidays and to acknowledge that this time of celebration puts us in touch with times of sadness and loss, of dreams not fulfilled, of safety not maintained, of disappointment and loss of faith. The very fact of gathering to talk about this was a statement of resilience and hope.

We made a small circle in front of the altar of the chapel. The gathering was scheduled to last about an hour and people were just beginning to talk when the door at the back of the chapel opened. A young man, probably twenty something, stood for a few seconds, then made his way to the front. "Who are you? What are you doing?" he asked.

Another few seconds of surprised silence. It seemed a question we might well have asked of him. Then the reply: "We're part of Emmanuel Church, and we're talking about the holidays. Some of us have some tough times around now."

"Well, can I stay?"

"Sure, you're welcome here."

The conversation resumed while each person was silently making evaluations of this extraordinary appearance. The man was neatly and warmly dressed, sober, quiet. He did not appear desperate in body or soul. But why was he here? What had brought him to us on this cold Thursday night when no service was scheduled? Our doors had just opened after weeks of being closed after the fire.

After about ten minutes, he spoke. "I have to go," he said. "If I kneel down in the middle of your circle, would you put your hands on my head and pray for me?" He paused for a few seconds and looked around. "My hair's pretty clean, but you could touch my shoulder if that feels better to you."

We looked at each other, and one of us replied, "Yes, we can do that."

We turned to our minister. "What's your name?" [the minister] asked. "What would you like us to pray for?"

He hesitated. "My name is Peter, and I wish I could like myself better," he said. He knelt and bowed his head. The people around the circle put their hands on his head and his shoulders. Our minister said a prayer for the young man, and the rest of us added ours, asking that he be kept safe, that he learn to value himself as surely as he is valued. We asked blessing upon him and gave thanks for his courage and his presence with us.

He stood and looked around the chapel and said, "Thank you. This may be the most important thing that ever happened to me."

Peter went out into the night. We will never know what brought him to us or what happened to him. His coming folded so smoothly into our gathering that it is only in the following days that we began to be aware of the depth of the gift he brought to us.

Peter's gift to Betsy and her companions was a gift of self. Their gift to him was a gift of presence. They were also willing to suspend their planned agenda to make space for an uninvited person's pain—no questions asked. Peter gave them his trust; they let go of their initial discomfort or irritation and received it. Because of the gifts Peter and the group were willing to make to each other, they received also the gift of spiritual presence that was not theirs to give or receive in a human exchange.

LIKING OURSELVES . . . AND EACH OTHER

The moment of truth in an encounter with strangers creates a bond of mutual humility, made possible through mutual vulnerability. In unspoken recognition that the Spirit blesses our interaction, we share something mystical, precious, and ineffable. Its power is available when we recognize and feel the bonds we have with all human beings, not because we have something to give one another but because if we can remove our defenses to give and receive from each other, the Spirit gives us this grace-imbued gift of human solidarity.

For me, for Betsy Bunn and her companions, and for anyone who is given the opportunity to be present for a stranger whose moment of truth brings him or her into our lives, there is also our own moment of truth. How easy it is to fortify ourselves against intrusion into our familiar circle—yes, even the circle of support we create with like-minded people in our religious or spiritual community. When someone enters our circle, particularly with a need, it is our usual response to want to help that person in some way. The moment of truth, however, is when we recognize our own helplessness—when the barrier crumbles between us (as the helpers) and them (as the ones in need of our help). Something inside us responds, not out of charity—though we may feel charitable—but in recognition of the human bond we share. Our compassion is more than loving-kindness or concern for the suffering of another person; it is rooted in the pain we share because we too know the place inside of ourselves that cries out for help.

"I want to like myself better." Yes, so do I. So do we all. Our moments of truth come when, recognizing aspects of our lives or our selves that inhibit our self-respect, we open our hearts to the transforming power of the Spirit, inviting the kind of change that results in our liking ourselves better.

Once, it was an improbable group of strangers who stirred me to consider how important it is that we learn to like ourselves better. In my first year of ministry in a congregation in Maryland, I decided I wanted to become more involved in the community. I wrote to several local organizations—service clubs, mostly—and offered my services as a speaker. I listed several possible topics, most of them dealing with social and ethical issues such as abortion or death with dignity. I made almost one hundred inquiries, but I received only two responses; one of those was from the county detention center. This was rather curious, as I had not sent the letter there. They had a group of prisoners who met weekly to hear speakers on special topics, and they scheduled me to come. In this diverse group of young people in their twenties, there were only a few women. Most of the students were serving a sentence for drug-related crime.

I was quite nervous as the heavy metal doors closed behind me after I had surrendered my keys and cleared security. I had led a fairly sheltered life—it did not include being locked inside the windowless concrete walls of a prison facility. Wondering what I could possibly have to say to these students, I gave my lecture on the ethical issues of abortion, and I invited discussion. Some of them participated, while others were demonstrably bored.

Then I led them in an exercise in values clarification.[2] Describing a man who had to make a decision regarding whether he would break the law to obtain a life-saving drug for his wife, I asked them to decide how they would deal with this ethical dilemma, and to give a reason for their decision. Students who had appeared disdainfully uninvolved became quite engaged (or enraged) as they discussed whether or not the man's love for his wife justified his stealing the drug that would save her life. Even the prison officials were impressed as they witnessed the lively discussion among the students, who seriously grappled with the moral dilemma in the situation. A few days later, they invited me to return regularly and continue with several sessions of values clarification discussion.

Although the composition of the group changed over the next several months as some of the prisoners completed their sentence or were transferred to another facility, we built a relationship of continuity and trust; the students learned to listen to one another with greater respect, even when they were in disagreement. On one occasion, I gave the students a list of several things they might want in their lives: good health, success, respect from others, wealth, popularity, love, freedom. I asked them to order the values according to which was most important, then to meet in groups and try to agree on a group ranking. They had a very difficult time coming to agreement on the group scale, except for the item at the top of the list. In every group, the item ranked first, above all else, was self-respect. It was even above freedom—and freedom gets a very high rating when you are in prison. What it came down to, as they put it was, "If you don't respect yourself, none of the rest of those things really mean anything."

Self-respect. It is the theme that recurs as I consider the nature of the moments of truth that I have related in this chapter. A man hits bottom and comes to my church to turn his life over to Jesus. Just what is the bottom, if not the place where he recognizes that his self-destructive behavior is a form of self-loathing, and that his self-loathing is a cry from his soul for self-respect? Self-respect demands change. Feeling powerless to change, and perhaps having alienated everyone who cares for him, he turns to a stranger, and a reluctant one at that, to mediate the love and power of God.

Similarly, it was self-respect that gave Peter the courage to ask a strange group of people to touch him and pray for him, and then to tell them how significant this event was for him. His gesture of reaching out was in itself an act of self-love and hope. His courage inspired them to shed their skepticism and let go of their expectations for the evening, thus drawing them into a circle where they could grow in their faith and their own self-love.

Self-respect is living your life not according to what others think but what you think and what you know is right. It is living life from the hub, from the spiritual center, where a grace abides. If you have this inner core of self-respect, then you live with a kind of freedom that is grounded in the Spirit, even if you are deprived of other freedoms. Victor Frankl, a psychiatrist who wrote of his experience in Nazi death camps, observed how some prisoners maintained their inner dignity even as they submitted to incredible humiliation and suffering. They retained the "last of human freedoms—to choose one's attitude in any given set of circumstances, to choose one's own way." He concluded, "It is this spiritual freedom—which cannot be taken away—that makes life meaningful and purposeful."[3] Maintaining dignity and self-respect is a matter of being true to yourself and the values you cherish, no matter what the circumstances.

The insight Frankl gained from his prison camp experience, though filtered through his scholarly research and his expertise as a psychotherapist, is really the same wisdom that emerged from my conversations with a group of young prison inmates, some of whom had dropped out of high school: "If you don't have self-respect, none of those other things will do much good."

Curious, isn't it, how we sometimes have to explore some of the prisons of our lives to discover what it means to be free?

CHAPTER TWO
BONDS OF FREEDOM

FOR A FEW YEARS, WHILE I WAS IN DIVINITY SCHOOL AT Harvard, I lived near Boston. During that time, I ran about forty miles a week. But I was a fair-weather runner, especially when temperatures dipped below thirty degrees Fahrenheit. I did not run on ice or snow.

It was after a week or two of snow and subfreezing weather—typical for a Boston winter—that a few springlike days thawed the ice and enticed me to resume my running routine. After the first half mile in the urban neighborhood that edged the Charles River, I came to the corner where I would frequently speak with a little old man holding a shopping bag. He really was a little old man with short stumpy legs that seemed to move not just forward but sideways, so that as he walked his body tipped a little to the right and then the left, with a slight hitch to one side. I saw him almost every day, coming back from his morning walk to the grocery store. We carried on a "running conversation" that consisted mostly of commentary on the weather. I had noticed that sometimes when I didn't see him going one way, I would pass him on the way back. He would be standing on the sidewalk in front of his house, holding his bag of groceries. I sometimes wondered if he was waiting for me to run by, especially when he said, "You're late today."

On that warm winter day after the snows, I actually heard him before I saw him. "Hey there! Where have you been?" he shouted from across the street. I smiled and waved. "Can't take the cold!" I explained, without changing my pace. "I've missed you!" he shouted, as I turned the corner.

He missed me! I said to myself. How about that? He missed me! I felt affirmed, and it did not really occur to me until some time later that my daily run had truly become something that this man had incorporated into his routine, too. It did not take much—a smile, a wave, a few friendly words, to give him some nourishment for the day. He had waited on the steps for me to pass on those days when I ran later; he also probably shopped more often than he needed to.

I never did find out his name. I never interrupted my run to stop and chat. But when the time came for me to move away, I let him know. It was the least I could do. He told me again he would miss me, and I believed him. I knew I would miss him, too.

SMALL GIFTS, BIG COMMITMENT

It is not unusual for us to encounter the same strangers almost daily as we follow a habitual routine of walking on the streets in our neighborhood. When I lived near an elementary school, my walking schedule coincided with latecomer school traffic. A friendly crossing guard brightened my mornings, for she always pushed the "walk" button when she saw me coming. The gesture was small, but it was acknowledgment of a personal connection and an expression of consideration. As she lifted her handheld stop sign and walked with me for a few yards, we reveled together in the freshness of the spring air or commiserated over the damp dreary days of winter. We would exchange brief reports on our inner weather, in response to the usual how-are-you query. In a few seconds each day, I learned that she was a grandmother, liked to garden, and participated in the AIDS Walk.

It was I who experienced missing this stranger when I arrived at the intersection one morning and she was not there. I greeted the substitute crossing guard with a friendly "Good morning!" He didn't smile back. He didn't press the "walk" button.

Assuming that the regular person was probably on vacation or out sick, I did not ask about her for a few weeks. Finally, I approached the man on patrol: "What happened to the woman who used to be at this intersection? Is she coming back?"

"I don't know," he said, flatly. "I think maybe she retired."

Still curious, I set out a little earlier one morning so that I could ask some of the parents and children at the intersection about the crossing guard. "Oh, you mean Norma," said one of the children. "Yeah, she was really nice. I think she moved." Another child, who also called her by her first name, speculated that she got sick and couldn't work anymore.

No one was able to offer an authoritative response, but all agreed that they missed Norma, who seemed to love helping kids get across the street safely and greeted everyone with the kind of smile that made them feel good inside.

Wherever she is, I hope Norma knows that how she greeted people during her morning patrol made a difference. Even on mornings when I left the house feeling grumpy, Norma had a way of helping me see past my own nose. Like the little old man who missed me, I was hungry for the attention that Norma offered when she smiled and pushed the "walk" button. Even her superfluous stop sign acknowledged and affirmed my presence.

These are the most ordinary of experiences. Most of us have numerous opportunities in the course of an average week to encounter strangers who become part of our lives in a tangential, but committed, way. The commitment is not the kind we may make to our family or friends or close neighbors; nor is it the same kind of loyalty we feel for people at work or in a religious community. It is a commitment to be present for other human beings—all of them—in a way that says that they matter. Just as I touched the life of a little old man, so Norma touched my life, and the lives of the children she escorted across the street. Dramatic? No. It is a subtle connection. But God is in the details, and in the daily human interaction we have with strangers.

It is as if, in our bonds with strangers, we have an unspoken covenant to care for one another as fellow human beings. In this context, to miss people we don't really know means that we miss something they offered into our days and into the world. It means missing something they gave to us when they smiled or carried on a superficial conversation. What we miss is not superficial at all, for it is a reminder of our need for human community and our common commitment to live with respect for one another. I missed Norma, just as the little old man with the shopping bag missed me. We were able to give something to one another that was nourishing to the soul and to our sense of being part of a larger human community. This kind of missing derives from gratitude for the meaningful ways we touch one another.

WHEN NEED BECOMES NEEDY

Sometimes, however, missing someone results more from need than gratitude; it can lead to creating barriers between people. We may think of need more in terms of our intimate relationships, but there is a common principle that applies to all relationships, from those we have with our pets to the relationship with the cosmic power that runs the universe. It has to do with accepting and receiving what another person (or being) offers without grasping for more than the person can give.

What if the little old man with the shopping bag had wanted me to stop and chat? If his need was so great that I couldn't get past without stepping on it, I probably would have started taking another route to avoid encountering him. He didn't want more than I could give, though, and it was my pleasure to give it. Nor did I want more from him than exactly what he gave me.

It is not uncommon for someone to overstep the boundaries (however undeclared they may be). Paula, a middle-aged woman living in a large metropolitan area, commuted a long distance to and from work. Since she had to make frequent stops to fill her gas tank, she found a local service station where she knew how to pump the gas and felt comfortable. She stopped there once or twice a week, early in the morning, freshly showered, coiffed, and "dressed for success" in a stylish suit, silk blouse, nylon stockings, and heels. She paid for her gas with cash, which required that she go to the booth and pay the attendant on duty. The attendant, a tall, attractive, muscular man at least fifteen years younger than she, came to recognize her, and they had friendly, noncommittal exchanges. Recalling how the acquaintance developed, she writes:

> After a while he started coming out of his little house to stand and talk with me as I pumped the gas. It turned out that he wrote poetry; he learned that I was an editor. So of course I said I'd like to see his poems, and one day he brought one to show me. I didn't attempt to edit it, but did type it up on my

computer and printed it out for him. I also corrected spelling where necessary. This went on for a few weeks, and was kind of fun. I was enjoying his poetry, and I think he liked seeing the nice clean printouts. Then things changed. He began incorporating me into his poems, making them close to love poems or fantasies. Whichever it was, I didn't want to know. I was sad at the change, and my manner toward him cooled. On the days I needed to stop for gas, I found myself going to my closet in search of my longest skirt and most modest blouse. Eventually I realized that I was just not comfortable going to that station anymore, and changed my morning fuel stop to a new location.

It is sad when a friendly and mutually satisfying relationship between strangers moves into the zone of inappropriate need. There is a dimension of commitment in our relationships with strangers, but it is not necessarily commitment to share from our private lives. It is, rather, commitment we make in the public realm, and it works best if we relate to one another with clarity about the boundaries operating in that domain. Sometimes, of course, a casual interaction with a stranger develops into a more intimate relationship; every friend or lover was, after all, once a stranger. Mutual attraction or common interest takes the relationship to another level. At every stage of relating, however, from the most casual to the most intimate, the health of the relationship depends, in part, on each person involved being able to care for the other's needs out of inner freedom and personal desire or ability to do so. When a relationship goes awry, there is sometimes one person who tends to expect or take, rather than invite and receive, what the other person has to give.

As a minister, I have often been in the position of reaching out to people in need. Most of the time, I can offer a caring presence for someone in pain, and how very rewarding that is for me, too. Once in a while, though, there is a person who needs more from me than it is within my role to give, and I may find myself avoiding that person. It would not matter what I offered; it would never be enough.

I have also been in the position of the one in need. Sometimes I go to the other extreme, which is to stay to myself when I should reach out a little more. The antidote to too much need is not isolation or withdrawal; nevertheless, that is often just what many of us do—withdraw. We put up a protective wall that says, in effect, "Do not try to touch me," and we are well defended against even the most sympathetic friend. Time after time, I hear about people who have withdrawn from their friends or associates during a time when they have been going through the pain of divorce or unemployment or personal crisis. Sometimes they become depressed. That, of course, is when they need friendship. Instead, they shut others out. It's tricky. I have just said that too much need is not conducive to healthy relationship. It may even frighten others and cause them to withdraw. So it should be no surprise when I say as well that many choose to isolate themselves in their most painful time. But that is not what I mean. The kind of need we feel in a time of transition is not the same as a general void that calls upon others to fill it.

What does it take to be vulnerable enough to invite a meaningful relationship where missing one another is the natural, healthy expression of human need, but not so vulnerable and needy that the missing speaks more of emptiness demanding that another person fill it? How do we make a commitment to each other where our needs are met without becoming an obstacle to healthy relationship?

RECEIVING WITHOUT GRASPING

The principle of being able to receive what another offers without grasping for more than the person can give applies to all relationships, from those we have with animals to the relationship we seek with the Spirit. Yes, we can ask more of a pet than the animal wants to give. We have a cat, for example, named Puppy Cat. She follows us around like a puppy. With no apparent physical needs, she cries for attention. She just wants to chat and demands confirmation that someone is listening. If anyone tries to pick her up, however, she protests. "Keep close and pet me," she says, "but don't hold me. I want to be free." Human beings are the same. "Love me," we say, "but do not intrude upon my personal identity." We want to be close, but we are afraid of being hurt. We need others, but we also want to be independent. We need to be needed, but we do not want to be used. If we can accept and understand these needs on the part of others, then we have taken a step toward being able to receive what they have to offer.

Our needs are most pronounced in a primary committed relationship, and they can be a common source of tension. Sometimes when I witness two people in a marriage or a partnership experiencing conflict, I am reminded of the vines that grow in my yard. Grapevines threaten to overwhelm a wisteria, which creeps into the forsythia. Over much of a fence, wild honeysuckle thrives, triumphant, even, over the poison ivy. Vines have a hard time living with other plants. They cling, they choke, and they pursue their own growth. They compete with each other. Properly pruned, they can live and let live. In fact, they can do better: they can thrive and bloom, thus having more to give.

Sometimes we act like vines—clinging, choking, and single-mindedly pursuing our own growth—and we need to be pruned. If we feel stifled or choked by another person's pursuit of growth, we tend to try to prune *him or her.* That never works. We need to cultivate a *self*-pruning mechanism, to check the urge to pursue our own growth without regard for the growing needs of others around us. This may require that we be coached in communicating our needs differently or listening more sensitively to the needs of another. Perhaps our attention turns to looking to a wider circle of people or activities to meet our needs so that we expect less.

Like a plant that is pruned, we discover our conscious trimming of our expectations renders more growth for ourselves as well as for our relationships. This does not mean we do not have needs; it means we consciously pare our expectations about what others will do to meet our needs.

A story from *Jacob the Baker* by Noah benShea, illustrates the wisdom of pruning our expectations:

> An older man, who was both wealthy and suspicious, invited Jacob to dinner in order to test him.
>
> When the dinner was served, Jacob was given an empty plate and cup while his host's plate overflowed and his cup had wine draining past its brim.
>
> Jacob said nothing but sat there and watched the man devour his sumptuous meal.
>
> When the man had finished, Jacob stood, said thank you for his dinner, and prepared to leave.
>
> Unable to resist Jacob's silence, the host asked, "Weren't you angry because I gave you nothing?"
>
> "No," said Jacob, passing through the door. "You gave me what you had. If I expected more from you than I received, then I was filled with my expectation and not your offer."[1]

It is unrealistic to imagine that we can or should, like Jacob, eliminate our expectations. This parable teaches that our needs are more likely to be satisfied if we do not ask more of others than their emotional resources give them the personal freedom to deliver. We, in turn, affirm our inner freedom, for it is we who determine whether or not we are pleased or disappointed.

THE BOND OF LOVE

One passage that couples frequently select to have read during their wedding ceremony is from Kahlil Gibran, whose prophet says, "Love one another, but make not a bond of love."

I think what Gibran really means is make not a *bondage* of love. This does not sound as poetic, but it makes a lot more sense. Love is, in fact, a bond—a bond in which we give freely of ourselves and nurture the growth of another. This bond of love is commitment.

When we encounter disappointment in a love relationship, it often has something to do with the loss of freedom—with the growth of this element of bondage that places conditions on our loving. The bondage destroys the bond.

We extol unconditional love. Have you ever heard any poetry about conditional love? Of course not. Not once have I performed a marriage ceremony where the couple vowed, "I will love you as long as you keep the house clean," or "I will love you as long as you stay sober," or "I will love you as long as you stay attractive to me." I have never heard a parent say, "I will love you as long as you make good grades," or "I will love you as long as you stay out of trouble," or "I will love you as long as you spend some time with me." No, we do not say these things, and we do not want to think that we feel them; but some of them become operative in our relationships nevertheless.

Sometimes love goes astray as we place conditions upon it, or as we allow the *bond* of commitment to become the *bondage* of commitment.

The bond of commitment honors the freedom of another person to be who he or she is; it also frees each of us to love without needing a particular response to our love.

This inner freedom derives from the same spiritual resources that empower us to choose how we respond to any circumstances in our lives. In Chapter One, I spoke of this freedom in relationship to self-respect. It is also out of this freedom that we respect others and *their* freedom to choose how they love. As Erich Fromm stated in his classic book *The Art of Loving,* there is no love that does not include respect for another, and respect "exists only on the basis of freedom. 'L'amour est l'énfant de la liberté,' as an old French song says; love is the child of freedom. . . ."[2] To respect others is to cherish their inner uniqueness and, while seeking to know them intimately, honor their mystery and their separateness. Any attempt to dominate them is a violation of this principle of loving. Our ability to offer our love freely and receive what someone has to give out of his or her freedom is a measure of the bond of mature love. Fromm reflects: "Infantile love follows the principle: *'I love because I am loved.'* Mature love follows the principle: *'I am loved because I love.'* Immature love says, *'I love you because I need you.'* Mature love says, *'I need you because I love you.'*"[3]

In the bond of love, then, love is freely given and received with respect for the other and a desire to respond to the needs of the other. The bondage of love, conversely, imprisons both giver and receiver in their own needs and is more likely to be expressed in terms of possessing the other. In the bond of love, our giving fills us with vitality and joy; in the bondage of love, our giving feels more like diminishment or self-sacrifice on another's behalf. The bond of love does not place conditions on how the other responds. The bondage of love does that, even though these conditions may exist only in our own heart rather than as a direct demand from another person. I don't think anyone is so virtuous as to be able to maintain a perpetual bond of loving, but to the extent that we strive for that purity in our loving, we feel a sense of harmony with the source of spiritual love that is grounded in freedom, generosity, and gratitude.

I think I have learned more about unconditional love in my role as a stepparent or surrogate mother than in any other relationship. I do not have biological children, but for several years my husband Chuck and I had one or two teenagers living with us. First it was Chuck's son, Brett; then Amy, our niece; then Tom, Chuck's younger son. By the time Amy went to college and Tom moved out to live on his own, I had invested a good bit of myself in my relationships with each of them. Our bonds, though not the same as those they had with their birth parents, were rooted in the tensions and affections of daily life. It was not always easy, but I tried not to expect more from them than they were able to give.

Brett went into the air force and then got married. After a few years, he and his wife announced that they were going to have a baby.

Chuck was going to be a grandfather! But what was I going to be? "Stepgrandma"? I suddenly came up against some difficult feelings. I had always felt that loving Brett, Tom, and Amy did not require that I be loved in return. I had managed for years to avoid getting into the martyr role (most of the time), but now I could feel some resentment building. Something about this new baby evoked many of the feelings I had worked so hard to transcend. Brett and his wife did not treat me as if I did not count; it was my own needs that interfered with my ability to join fully in the joyful anticipation of this birth. As I became aware of the inner obstacles and removed them, I finally allowed myself to become a grandparent, without being so conscious of my second-class status.

The baby was born in Germany, and it did not take long for me to become quite smitten with being *Oma*. But the more attached I became to my granddaughter, Jennafer, the more I found I still had to deal with some of my less noble feelings. It was Chuck, not I, who had the legitimate claim to grandparent status. Me, I was just a grandmother by marriage. So I found myself wishing, sometimes, that I were a "real" grandparent. In addition, one of Jennafer's other grandparents lived in the same city with her, while I was several hundred miles away. That grandparent, who ascribed to many of the beliefs of the radical religious right, held values quite contrary to mine. At one point, when Jennafer was about four, she said something to me that reflected her other grandmother's judgments. I found myself feeling jealous toward the grandmother who lived near Jennafer and had more influence in her life.

In some ways, my jealousy was well founded. But I had to recognize that I had made choices for my life that did not include living in close proximity to my grandchild. Also, I came to realize that the jealousy I felt toward this grandparent and the other "real" grandparents was diminishing my love for Jennafer. It was shrinking my heart. That is what jealousy does. It shrinks your heart.

Maya Angelou compares jealousy in a relationship to salt in food. "A little can enhance the savor, but too much can spoil the pleasure and, under certain circumstances, can be life-threatening."[4] Too much jealousy, like too much need, takes the freedom out of loving. In Shakespeare's tragedy of Othello, jealousy was indeed deadly. It was the green-eyed monster that destroyed Othello's trust in his beloved Desdemona. Or, as I once heard someone express it, it is "the dragon that slays love under the pretense of keeping it alive." It implies that you only have so much love to give, and you must give it all to one person. It quantifies love. It erodes trust. It makes a bondage of love.

The most rewarding relationships, of course, are those where there is a commitment to mutual unconditional love—where mature adults are able to nurture each other's growth in a bond of freedom. In love, we lose ourselves to find ourselves. There it is again, this spiritual paradox, this bond of freedom. We give up some of our autonomy as we bond with one another, yet we gain grounding in something larger than ourselves or our own needs. I have heard God defined as the freedom that allows other freedoms to exist. Anne Morrow Lindbergh describes the power of love in similar terms:

People talk about love as though it were something you could give, like an armful of flowers. And a lot of people give love like that—just dump it down on top of you, a useless strong-scented burden. I don't think it is anything you can give . . . love is a force in you that enables you to give other things. It is the motivating power. It enables you to give strength and freedom and peace to another person. It is not a result; it is a cause. It is not a product; it produces. It is a power, like steam or electricity. It is valueless unless you can give something else by means of it.[5]

No matter whether it is for a friend or a lover or a child or a parent, or even the love we feel for a stranger, love is an expression of our bond with the Spirit. All love, writes Fromm, springs from our human experience of separateness and the resulting need to overcome the anxiety of separateness by the experience of union. Ultimately, our hungry spirits seek union with Spirit or God, and with perfect love. This love is both the freedom that allows other freedoms to exist and the power that fuels our giving. Our love is like an invisible line stretched between human hearts and linking them with the Spirit.

We maintain the bond of freedom when we neither make demands for more than others can offer nor allow their needs to dictate how we love them. This bond is the freedom out of which we offer our affection and attention to others unconditionally; it is also the freedom that empowers us to allow others to be and become themselves.

AN UNCONDITIONAL BOND AMONG STRANGERS

I return now to the commitment we have to strangers, and I wonder if there might be a mutual unconditional love that we cultivate on a different level with them. Does this bond with people whom we do not even know affect how we relate to our most intimate companions?

I think it does. If we can achieve a balance in our relationships with strangers whereby some of our needs for affirmation are met appropriately, then I think we are better able to give and receive from our closest friends and family within the bonds of freedom and healthy relationship. But if we go through an entire day, for example, without meeting up with anyone like Norma the cheerful crossing guard (and instead perhaps encountering people who are abrupt, rude, or dismissive), we are likely to need more from the people who are committed to us; we are prone to push the boundaries on those relationships. If we can receive more of what we need by making a commitment to civil exchanges with strangers, I think we will have more realistic expectations with regard to a committed relationship with a partner, family member, or close friend.

Consider, for instance, exchanges that take place in the bank or the grocery store. I often choose to make a bank deposit using the drive-through option. But even if I am parked twenty feet away from the teller, with several layers of glass, post, and vacuum-thrust equipment between us, I appreciate the friendly greeting I receive from the face behind the glass. I may not even see the smile, but I know it is there. I can hear it in her electronically garbled voice. I need that. I appreciate it. My day would be deficient if I did not get it.

Grocery clerks in my neighborhood are not inclined to include the friendly bonus. They offer an initial perfunctory greeting and then start scanning and punching the numbers. Sometimes, they don't even make eye contact. I spoke recently with someone who remarked about the difference it makes when she shops at Trader Joe's, a chain of earth-friendly discount grocery stores based on the West Coast of the United States. There, she tells me, the internal (or intimate) relations of the company are all about valuing employees highly and promoting those who want to grow with the organization. Starting with their own "family" of workers, they treat everyone as if they matter. The commitment extends to their relations with the public. Young people are hired for their desire to engage with customers. That's a qualification for getting a job at Trader Joe's—you have to like talking with strangers. So when she shops there, she leaves with a "pleasant endorphin feeling"—a sensation that is both physical and spiritual, and imbued with affirmation. In short, she feels valued, not just as a customer but as a human being.

Sure, business is business, but some companies practice principles of human community that are more than good business; they produce a ripple effect. If I shop at Trader Joe's, for example, I return home or to work feeling affirmed. On the other hand, if I trade in a store where my mere presence appears to be burdensome to the weary clerk on duty,

I move on to my next interaction in a less content frame of mind. In a highly impersonal society, this constant cascading of cold and unfeeling encounters creates a hardened mind-set that closes us off to each other and to Spirit, even if we don't want to be closed off.

This is not to say that I do not have needs that can only be met by my intimate companions. Perhaps, however, I will need less from them (and expect less from them) if I give and receive affirmation among strangers. Maybe then I will be freer to receive what they give, and will receive it gratefully. This generates a cycle whereby a balanced dynamic of need and expectation in my close relationships also renders me present when I encounter strangers.

HOSPITALITY AS A WAY OF BEING

To be present with strangers is an expression of hospitality, a value practiced in many religious traditions. For Christians, hospitality is central. It is, according to writer Parker Palmer, the "one word above all others that suggests the quality we should seek in meeting with strangers."[6] For those of us who think of hospitality as something we *do* to welcome others into our space, Palmer expands it to convey an expression of who we *are* in relationship to one another. Chapter Eight explores the notion of hospitality in greater depth, but I introduce it here in its broadest context, as part of our commitment to live in a way that is consistent with our spiritual values. "Hospitality," writes Palmer, "means inviting the stranger into our private space, whether that be the space of our own home or the space of our personal awareness and concern." We express our values, then, by creating a hospitable space wherever we are. An inhospitable space is one where people "feel invisible—or visible but on trial. A hospitable space is alive with trust and good will, rooted in a sense of our common humanity."[7]

Our commitment, then, is to create a hospitable space, a space that says in many ways that the stranger is affirmed and accepted. Affirmation and acceptance are, after all, two needs most basic to the human spirit. Another is attention—being present for each other.

Our spiritual imperative is to give attention to one another in a way that respects freedom and personal space. Hospitality does not require that shy people be gregarious; it suggests that they be *present* in a way that is comfortable for others. A friend of mine describes her demeanor while traveling, for example, as assuming "airplane face." Airplane face is a declaration of space, not a barrier of incivility. Conscious of the person seated next to her, she is friendly and hospitable, but she is also clear about wanting a few precious hours while in transit to read or get some work done. Being present to others does not require that she engage in two hours of intense conversation, but she is likely to be attentive when the window passenger needs to get out, and she does not recline her chair as far as it goes if there is someone behind her whose comfort would be compromised. There are small but significant ways in which those around her are visible, not invisible.

As we grow in our ability to receive and respond to others in a bond of freedom and commitment, we grow also in our relationship with the Spirit. Spirit means breath. Nothing is more natural than breathing. But in this age of consumer religion, you can walk into any bookstore and find dozens of how-to books on being spiritual. Hardly a week passes that I do not talk to someone wanting more spirituality in his or her life. People go to a minister for spirit the way they go to a doctor to get a prescription; they would like to have a spirit pill to take before going to bed. Like the doctor who wants to prescribe the right medicine, I find myself wishing I had something on the shelf I could hand them and say, "Here, try this, and call me in five days." I might as well try to bottle the air we breathe.

Yes, there are books to help us learn spiritual disciplines, and wisdom aplenty with regard to addressing our inner obstacles to spiritual health. They are all helpful, even if they do no more than remind us to slow down and pay attention to the present moment. But no amount of reading, meditating, praying, or even attendance at worship services will give us what the Spirit intends for us to give to one another. *We* are the mediators of the Spirit—this is what it means to be hospitable, and our prayer and meditation empowers us to offer holy presence in the world. Attention, affirmation, and acceptance: each of these is a human need that can be addressed through our hospitality toward one another.

To be human is to be hungry each day for a smile, for a touch, for words of affirmation, and for a sense of connection and meaning. If the Spirit speaks to us, it is in our everyday interactions—encounters with strangers and friends, neighbors and family. It is in the voice of loneliness and need, and in the voice of love and freedom. It is in our struggles with jealousy and our hunger for meaning.

To live in the embrace of the Spirit requires that we reach out to others without grasping and receive from others without expectation. It is as simple, and as complex, as breathing.

If the Spirit speaks to us, it is in our everyday interactions—encounters with strangers and friends, neighbors and family. It is in the voice of loneliness and need, and in the voice of love and freedom. It is in our struggles with jealousy and our hunger for meaning.

CHAPTER THREE
CLOSE TO HOME

It was my first occasion to attend the large annual gathering of Unitarian Universalists from the United States, Canada, and outposts around the world. Excited to be among others of my faith, I approached the crowded vestibule of hotel elevators, curiously scanning the name badges, buttons, and ribbons that offered bits of information about fellow delegates. I had already met some interesting people on previous elevator excursions, and as I pressed the "up" button, I smiled at others who were gathering.

It was a long time before any of the six lifts in operation stopped. While we waited, more delegates gathered as the morning workshops dispersed. Finally, the light on one of the buttons went out and a familiar "ding!" created frenzy as everyone herded in the direction of the available elevator. Even the first to claim their positions, however, were disappointed, as a chorus of passengers already in the elevator thrust the palms of their hands toward us and announced, "Sorry, no room!" I could see that there was space enough for a few more people, but the incumbent riders were quick to inform us that the elevators in this hotel were easily overloaded and were not performing reliably.

A few more loaded lifts passed me up before I finally boarded my ride to the sixteenth floor, feeling nervous by this time about the potential for technical malfunction.

A man in the corner of the crammed cubicle struck a match and lit a cigarette. Another man verbally pounced on him. "Put that out!" he demanded. "Can't you see the sign there? No smoking on the elevator!"

The smoker took a long deep drag on his cigarette and said nothing.

"You are not allowed to smoke here," repeated the other. "Put it out!"

"No, I will not," said the smoker.

They went back and forth like this as the elevator stopped to discharge or take on passengers, and they were still sparring when I got off. I was relieved to leave the smoky elevator. I was more relieved to escape the rising tension as these two mounted an unpleasant standoff. Here I was at a convention of people who were passing resolutions about addressing human rights in Central America, but we who witnessed this acrimonious encounter didn't seem to have the resources to deal with a dispute over smoking in an elevator.

The man was right, of course: there was no smoking allowed in the elevators. I will always wonder, however, if he might have gotten another response if he had been less hostile in his initial confrontation. It is hard to distinguish who was the worse offender: the man puffing on his cigarette, or the person who rudely invoked the rules rather than personally addressing the recalcitrant smoker.

To what extent were the rest of us—the innocent bystanders—failing to live up to our responsibility to call them both to task in the name of our common religious values? I like to think that if I were to relive those few minutes in the elevator, I would behave differently. But what would that look like? Perhaps no more than a statement of my discomfort with a conversation of this nature taking place among people of faith; even that would have been better than silently allowing the quarrel to escalate.

We who shared a common religious community did not have the resources for dealing with a confrontation, so it is not surprising that most conflicts among strangers, even those who appear to have a foundation for community, either develop into an unpleasant altercation or find their way to the legal arena. Although we have rules about things like not smoking in an elevator, we do not have the social contract whereby we can deal with what happens when someone breaks the rules.

FROM HANDSHAKE TO SUBPOENA

In his book *Bowling Alone,* Robert Putnam observes that since 1970 the legal profession has undergone a massive expansion, with the major portion of the increase resulting from a demand for formal agreements to replace those that had, in years previous, been sealed with a handshake: "Almost imperceptibly, the treasure that we spend on getting it in writing has steadily expanded since 1970, as has the amount that we spend on getting lawyers to anticipate and manage our disputes. In some respects, this development may be one of the most revealing indicators of the fraying of our social fabric. For better or worse, we rely increasingly—we are forced to rely increasingly—on formal institutions, and above all on the law, to accomplish what we used to accomplish through informal networks reinforced by generalized reciprocity—that is through social capital."[1] *Social capital* "refers to connections among individuals—social networks and the norms of reciprocity and trustworthiness that arise from them."[2] (Putnam's title derives from his witness to the veritable demise of such associations as bowling leagues and civic associations, where people develop a sense of their place in the context of a larger social identity.) The shift from handshake to subpoena results from a marked decline in social capital in the last few decades of the twentieth century.

YOUR DOG IS KILLING MY GRASS

I spoke recently with a friend, Ann Lewis, about this disturbing trend toward reliance on formalized recourse for approaching conflict with neighbors. As president of the board of directors for a humane society in a midsized city, she immediately identified with my concern. Ann is also a journalist, and she sent me some observations from an interview she conducted with the executive director of the humane society in a small city:

> Shelly A. Moore has over eighteen years of law enforcement experience in the field of animal control and sheltering. More and more she finds a public unwilling or unable to deal directly with their neighbors in areas of conflict. "People are always quick and ready to take the path of least resistance in any area of a contentious nature," says Moore. "They want someone else to do it for them." This attitude usually means phoning animal control at the least provocation rather than dealing with a neighbor that they usually do not even know.
>
> This anonymous form of communication follows through the process. "We have a noise ordinance in this city which includes nuisance barking of dogs. Our animal control can give a citizen the tools to resolve the situation, but the ordinance requires that the one offended, the person who hears the continual noise, must be the one to go to court. However, nearly to a person, the citizens want us to take care of it, and become distressed when we cannot provide them with an easy way out."
>
> Moore, a "baby boomer" herself, lays the blame at that generation's "I want what I want and I want it now" attitude of instant gratification. Add to that a technology that has alienated us from interpersonal relationships. People now use a computer for their companionship where once they might have sat on the front porch greeting passing neighbors—so you find an element of the human condition that seems to be lost. Moore thinks that we have misplaced a degree of knowledge of how to get along with one another.

A transient society is also to blame. People are more willing and financially able to move around, again perhaps looking for that perfect geographical gratification. The importance of long-time friends and neighbors is an unknown or unneeded component of their lives. With both adults in a household generally working all day, bedroom communities of the suburbs are just that: a place to sleep. This leads to a low tolerance for any irritant, including a neighbor's wayward animals.

Many times an animal complaint is just the tip of a large iceberg of minor irritants between people who do not know each other, yet live nearby. "Calling law enforcement is a mechanism to cause chaos for someone," she says. Animal control officers all know that there is usually something else going on in the tenuous relationship between people. "There is a lot of anger out there," Moore adds. "Complainants don't want to give us their names for fear of retaliation." And in fact, the usual first response to a complaint is not concern for causing a problem, or a proffered solution, but "who called you?"

Moore has found a lot of merit in mediation sessions, and in fact this is sometimes the only way to get neighbors to speak to one another and seek solutions to their conflict.

Many cases do not make it to mediation because one party or the other is often not motivated to try to resolve the situation. In other cases—the ones more likely to reach mediation—all parties are motivated to resolve the situation.

Take the case of the Great Dane. When Ruth Gable moved to western North Carolina, she bought a home in the country with a nice view of the mountains and few neighbors nearby. A professional writer, she worked from her home. She had difficulty working, however, because of the persistent barking of her neighbors' Great Dane. When Ruth spoke to her neighbors, Bobby and Susan McFlint, and told them that the dog was interrupting her work, they were sympathetic, but the dog continued to bark. Finally, Ruth called animal control. Two officers visited the McFlints and discussed the situation. Embarrassed at "having the law called on them" and guessing that Ruth was the one who called animal control, Bobby called her and yelled at her over the phone. Feeling frightened, frustrated, and nearly desperate, Ruth called a friend who suggested she try mediation.

After several discussions with Mediation Center staff, Ruth and the McFlints agreed to meet with two mediators to attempt to resolve the conflict. Both sides expressed strong feelings about the situation, but after about an hour of quarreling, they worked out a solution whereby the McFlints agreed to keep their dog quiet in the early morning when Ruth liked to write. In the afternoon, Ruth agreed to do things at home that didn't require total quiet or to write somewhere else. If there were future problems, the neighbors agreed they would try to work it out themselves, or come back to mediation.[3]

BARKS, BITES, AND BOUNDARIES

This account of the barking dog and Shelly Moore's observations are consistent with what I have observed in the diverse settings where I have lived over the past ten years. Whether I lived in a metropolitan area, a suburb, a small city, or a rural village, I noted reluctance on the part of neighbors of all generations to speak directly with one another when there was the threat of conflict involved. People who were angry with their neighbors for failing to clean up after a dog on the sidewalk in the city, for example, would write angry letters to the newspaper rather than speak to the offenders. Perhaps because there has been a diminishment of social capital, and we have no common agreements about how to approach conflict in a civil manner, most of us have less investment in developing a relationship with a neighbor or stranger that might include more direct personal communication. Not knowing who we are dealing with, we cannot know how they might respond; our attempt to confront them may trigger a hostile, or even violent, response. Feeling unsafe, or perhaps foolish and unskilled in dealing with an unpleasant encounter, we tend to avoid the situation. We do not have a common sense of what is at stake for us all, so we lack the willingness to risk feeling clumsy or provoking aggression in order to create community among strangers.

An experience I had several years ago—coincidentally involving several dogs—presents itself as a parable for thinking about how we approach issues with our neighbors.

I live in a rural area where narrow roads—some paved, some gravel—wind through valleys where you see cornfields and vacation resorts, cow barns and horse ranches, mobile homes and summer retreats. During the past few decades, the countryside has become inhabited by a curious blend of upscale professionals who listen to National Public Radio and residents who tune their radios to country or gospel music. Although I fall more in the former category, many of the friends I have made and kept over the years, even when I was only a summer resident, are in the latter.

I have never cared for the appearance of most mobile homes, but I have seen how young people struggle to find a place where they can afford to live. Parents may give them a little piece of the front yard (which might be several acres) upon which they place their mobile home. Some of the long aluminum boxes have gradually been camouflaged. First a peaked roof, then a room added on in front, then, finally, wood siding to cover the whole thing. A tidy yard is edged with zinnias planted from seed. A vegetable garden always yields enough zucchini and tomatoes to feed the neighbors.

Almost every family in this part of the country has at least one dog. Most dog owners don't have fences and wouldn't think of keeping their pets tied up. I love dogs—we have always had at least one or two large ones in our family—so I tend to be tolerant of them.

Although I am a walker now, there was a time when I ran my way through the valley. I was not generally bothered when dogs barked at me or chased me to the edge of their territory. I could usually fend them off by stomping my foot, saying their name, and shouting, "Go home!" I tried this tactic on one occasion, however, without success. I was being chased this time not by one dog but by three or four. Not having seen these dogs before, I suspected there was a bitch in heat not far away.

Before I knew it, a few more mongrels joined them and there was a pack at my heels. A Saint Bernard (the only one I could identify as any particular breed) nipped at my hand, and about the time I realized these animals did not want to play, one of the small hybrids took a serious bite out of my calf. With blood running down my leg and into my shoe, I limped the remaining half-mile home, still in shock and shaking with the terror of attack.

The injury healed and I eventually recovered to run again. The first day out, I encountered two neighbor dogs I had passed many times before without incident. They barked (as always) and chased me (as always). But the terror of having been attacked choked away my usual response. Instead of telling the animals to return home in my firm and confident manner, I shrieked at them to go away, my voice high-pitched with fear. They pursued me into a ditch beside the road, and I twisted my ankle.

For a while, I avoided running on the roads. I stuck to repeating the half-mile of private road that led up to our house. There I was safe. Safe and restless. My own driveway began to feel like a self-constructed prison of fear.

So I returned to the road. This time, however, I carried a stick. As I approached the same dogs that had pursued me into the ditch I waved the stick at them and, as if it were a magic wand, they miraculously retreated.

I was free to enjoy my run once again. It really bothered me, though, to have to carry the stick. Even though I never intended to use it—or at least hoped I would not need to—I felt less fearful. No, not less fearful: I felt more in control. In fact, as I waved my stick at the neighbor dogs—those dogs that had driven me into a ditch—I sort of enjoyed watching them retreat.

As I said, I love dogs. Under other circumstances, I would probably even like the dog that bit me. I suspect that the dogs are afraid, too. Who knows what prompts their aggression? Perhaps the neighbor dogs seriously believed I was trespassing in their territory, a threat to their home and their honor.

We each defended ourselves. We didn't understand each other's needs or each other's fears. We just had our common language, the language of self-defense, territorial definition, and protection.

I call this a parable. That's because it started me thinking about things like barks and sticks—mainly about all the barks and sticks that we use in our relationships with our neighbors, usually in place of a direct personal conversation about territorial issues that may concern us. For example, when some new neighbors built a house where I had enjoyed a nice view of the woods, I didn't like it one bit. I valued my privacy. So I put up a screen of white pine trees that would eventually grow up between our two properties (white pines, because they grow fast). I had nothing against my neighbors, but they really had no way of knowing that I was barking at their house, not at them.

A few years later, however, as the trees began to restrict my neighbor's view of the mountains, I realized I had constructed more than a privacy screen. My bark had an unintentional bite to it, and the trees had become a symbol of estrangement. I finally spoke with them, and told them to feel free to trim the pines back as they needed. Eventually, I agreed to take the trees out altogether. Since that time, we have bonded as neighbors, exchanging beans for tomatoes and even tractor time for backhoe expertise. My husband recently put up a horse barn near the property line, but before he broke ground he checked with the neighbors to be sure they did not object.

RESTRICTIONS AND COVENANTS

My encounter with the aggressive dogs occurred many years ago, before real estate developers discovered my rural neighborhood. During the last fifteen years or so, as small farmers have given up their formerly lucrative tobacco allotment and sold off the land, dozens of restricted communities have supplanted the working farms. These developments have good roads (not dirt and gravel) and the power lines are underground. The main thing, though, is that they don't allow mobile homes, and people can't leave old washing machines, refrigerators, or pickup trucks in the yard to rust. Sometimes I think I would like to live in one of those restricted communities, because someone else has already waved the stick to maintain a standard of acceptable appearance in their territory. All the neighbors are alike in their appreciation of a view unblemished by things like a pile of tires or an aluminum outbuilding. All the fences, if fences are allowed, are usually alike—split rail or something like that (no chain link). I wouldn't be surprised if there wasn't some kind of rule about having dogs tied up or on a leash, too. There are definite advantages to the restricted neighborhood.

But you don't see too many gardens there, with rows and rows of sunflowers taller than the corn. Neighbors won't be able to tell you much about the history of the creek that runs through your property. If you get into one of those developments where the bark and the stick are right there at the entrance, on a nice tasteful wooden sign that says something like "Shadycrest Mountain Estates—A Restricted Community," chances are you will always keep a good distance between you and the neighbors who live in the unrestricted sections. It's likely you won't even know each other or begin to understand each other when there's a town meeting to discuss zoning, and you will probably do a lot of barking and stick waving without getting through to one another. I've seen it happen, particularly in communities that are growing and becoming gentrified. The newcomers want to keep the land beautiful and unspoiled; the farmers and long-time residents want a place where their children can afford to put up a little home and raise a family. To a certain extent, the newcomers have more money and more education. But not always. Sometimes what it comes down to is nothing but a different way of life. As Wendell Berry puts it, to one it is the *views* of the land that matter most; to another it is the *use* of the land that is more important.

Berry's description of a Vermont farmer's perspective identifies some of the issues that arise for us. The farmer, David Budbill, wrote to Berry: "What I've noticed around here with the militant ecology people (don't get me wrong, I, like you, consider myself one of them) is a syndrome I call the Terrarium View of the World: nature always at a distance, under glass." Budbill noted that the "eco-folks" would buy land and post it, thinking they would just protect the animals and enjoy looking at the scenery. "They think they're protecting the environment, even though they've forgotten, or never knew, that nature abhors a vacuum . . . and in a couple of years their meadow is full of hardhack and berries and young gray birch and red maple." By posting their property, the "upper-class eco-folks" were alienating neighbors who had previously permitted others on their land: ". . . we always, with our neighbor, pick apples in the fall off the trees on a down-country owner's land. There is a feeling we have the *right* to do that, a feeling that the sin is not trespass, the sin is letting the apples go to waste." Budbill then registered his strongest complaint: "The Audubon types (I'm a member of Audubon) are fighting . . . terribly hard to zone trailers out of areas like this. . . . Well, a trailer is the only living space a working man around here can afford. There are so many elements of class struggle lying under the attitudes of a lot of environmentalists. . . ."[4]

The cultural gap this farmer described in the 1970s persists into a new century. Although I have plenty of dirt under my fingernails, I am more of a views person—more like the eco-folks; but I don't really want to isolate myself from the neighbors who are different from me. Of course, I would only be fooling myself if I thought we could just ignore our differences, but I have found that once we can each get past some of our prejudice, we have plenty to talk about. I don't mean just the weather or how bad the Japanese beetles and ticks are this year. I mean things that are common to every human being, no matter how rich or poor or how conditioned by life in the city or the country or the suburbs: things like delight in the wildflowers and the hummingbirds; things like family squabbles and losses, living with teenagers and being grandparents, past memories and future dreams. It doesn't even hurt to gossip a bit about other neighbors, as long as our gossip isn't meant to be a stick we hold up together so we can shut the others out.

What happens when we spend time just being neighbors is that we begin to see how the others think. I don't mean we agree with each other. I don't mean we become close friends, even. We just get a little better idea what it is like to see life through a different lens from our own. I have a feeling we are more likely to be able to listen to one another if we end up in a town meeting to discuss zoning issues. Not only do we care about them and listen with respect for who they are, but we are apt to frame our questions or comments in an informed and civil manner—avoiding accusations or judgments that escalate, rather than temper, divisiveness.

When it comes to building social capital, we can make a lot of headway in our own backyard.

GETTING UP THE NERVE TO SAY IT

Being a good neighbor takes some effort, especially when you live, as I do, where zoning laws are minimal. Our county government passed an ordinance against leaving abandoned cars on private property, but it has not legislated against cluttering the land with derelict houses, mobile homes, trucks, or city buses. These are a few of the larger items that were stored on a lot adjacent to our property when we relocated permanently to North Carolina. A frame house that was moved onto the property about ten years before was still propped on cement blocks. We were encouraged when one of the three abandoned mobile homes that occupied the lot was disassembled and taken away. But nothing else was cleared. The weeds in summer grew through the slats of the rusty mobile home frame. Nearby, several tires, a washing machine, and a seatless toilet formed a cluster of rotting rubber, chipped enamel, and porcelain.

Apart from being a blot on the landscape, this collection of rusting carcasses and broken glass was a health hazard. Recalling how I loved to explore vacant buildings when I was a child, I worried about children getting hurt, or perhaps encountering the snakes or rats that had surely taken up residence in this heap of neglect.

Like other neighbors who decried this eyesore, I was unsure of how to approach getting it cleaned up. When the subject came up in conversation among us, we agreed that the property owner, an amicable person, did not mean to offend us, and we understood that he lived and worked at a distance from our road. Several people suggested that we contact county authorities in the hope of getting some action. That seemed to be the easiest way, but it troubled me to call in the officials before first trying to communicate with the neighbor. Although many of us had spoken with the owner or one of his sons, there had not been any joint effort in the neighborhood to get something done. This appeared to be the next step.

Although I have voted for zoning restrictions that would eliminate this sort of dilemma, I also realize that the circumstances of this situation forced me and other neighbors to relate to the problem less formally. Without a legal avenue of communication, we were challenged to confront the situation in a manner that would be in accordance with our desire to treat our neighbor with courtesy and respect, no matter how offended we were by the condition of his property.

I drafted a letter to the property owner and circulated it among neighbors for their signatures. The letter did not indicate that we would call the authorities if he did not respond; it was my hope that we would not have to use any threats of that nature. Some of us were also prepared to assist him with the cleanup effort. Our appeal was to his desire to be responsive to his neighbors. It was my plan then to try to set up a time when I could speak with him and share the letter with him.

After about two weeks, two other families had signed the letter; I spoke with two more who wanted to talk directly with the landowner. Meanwhile, I had made several attempts to call him and gotten no answer or message machine. Finally, I caught him at home on a weekend and told him that many of us were hoping he would be cleaning up the property soon. Then I asked if he had plans to do further cleanup; he said he intended to get started in a month or so. At that point, it seemed best to wait on giving him the letter. It had already prompted some other neighbors to speak with him, and I thought that if enough of us let him know how much it bothered us, he might be inspired to get to it within a few months.

It was not a month before the work began. In fact, it was only a few days. Meanwhile, I spoke with another neighbor or two and began to learn more about this nonresident neighbor with whom I was only barely acquainted myself. Words like "wise" and "kind" kept coming up as they spoke of a man who had been a single custodial parent and worked hard to provide for his children. In my own brief conversations with him, my appreciation for his authenticity and his sense of humor grew. No longer was he the neighbor with the junk heap on his property; he was a man for whom I felt admiration and respect.

At this point, I realized I would not be able to send the letter. Entering the conversation with this man and other neighbors, however, had begun a process of communication that called all of us into a space where we faced our fears of confrontation at the same time that we recognized the need to speak directly to him, not gossip among ourselves and write letters to county officials. I think we recognized that the letter could set up a dynamic whereby we were on a self-righteous mission and he was bound to be embarrassed rather than inspired toward consideration of his neighbors. I also learned a few things about the meaning of the word *patience.* The cleanup was proceeding, but it was not on my schedule. It was going to be many months before we would see the project completed. Meanwhile, there would also be more opportunities to get to know a neighbor who was a fine human being.

My neighborhood is my classroom, and my teacher is the Spirit, calling me to take a few risks and get beyond my fear and discomfort. Since the owner of the offensive collection of derelict dwellings and vehicles did not live on the property in question and was not someone I knew, it would have been easy to avoid getting involved with him or any other neighbors. Believe me, I considered it. Like most people, I avoid conflict if I can. Like the people who call animal control officers and seek to be anonymous, I was tempted to call the county health department and ask them to take care of the problem. I really did not want to take on a confrontation. It was not retaliation that I feared from this kind and gentle man; it was that my neighbor would misunderstand my motive and think me hostile or aggressive. A nudge from the Spirit pushed me to get beyond my concern for what someone else thought of me and consider what I thought of myself, or what I would think of myself if I hid behind the actions of a government agency.

But this was not just about my own struggle to do the right thing. It was about a vision of community among people; it was about what it means to be a neighbor.

It comes out of the same vision we have for our close relationships. All of us who live in a family (including families that do not share the same residence) become acquainted with our own ways of dealing with conflict and communication. Our home is our classroom too. There are times when we prefer to write a letter rather than speak face-to-face, perhaps because we fear another person's anger. We catch ourselves engaging in passive-aggressive behavior. Instead of saying, for example, that we really want others to be more considerate about where they leave their clothing, we shove it in the corner of the closet. There is no disputing that most of the trouble we have with talking to our neighbors is not unlike the trouble we have talking with our intimate companions. Getting past the obstacles on the property line isn't so different from getting up the nerve to talk to our own kin.

REVIVING THE SPIRIT OF THE BLOCK PARTY

The neighborhood in which I grew up was an old-fashioned one where people gathered on the Fourth of July for a cookout (usually at our house), baseball, badminton, horseshoes, and homemade ice cream. When a new family moved onto our street, they were greeted with plates of freshly baked cookies and information about where to shop for the best produce. Parents took care of each other's children, and teenage boys took turns mowing lawns for the older people. As a child, I learned to knit from Em Hudson and treasured the pink organdy dress that Gay Stamp made for me when she found out how envious I was of Peggy and Dorothy Rosene's Easter dresses. Being on Cartwright Street meant that I knew the old people and the single folks, not just the families with children. My parents were atheists, so we did not have a faith community; but we did have a community.

There are still neighborhoods like mine, of course, but they are surely less the norm than they were when I was growing up in the 1950s. It is now a rare person who grows up in one area and stays there, surrounded by the same neighbors for fifteen or twenty years. Living in a mobile society, we have to cultivate new neighbors throughout much of our lives.

In all of my adult life, I have become acquainted with many of my neighbors, but selectively; it is sometimes several months before I meet someone in the house, condominium, or apartment right next door to mine. There are fewer women at home these days to bake the cookies or send the children down to visit with an elderly widow; there is also not an ethic of being present for neighbors. It takes some effort just to know your neighbor's name, let alone create a sense of community among those who share the same street, building, or road.

Most of us are not inclined to remove the impediments, within ourselves and in our culture, that prevent us from having a relationship with our neighbors. We seek out our experience of community, instead, in a religious community or secular organization. In most cases, we are drawn toward a gathering of people who are like us; we join the bridge club, an athletic league, a parent-teacher association, and the like.

As Robert Putnam points out, all of these groups, whether they are oriented toward civic service or recreation or lifestyle affinity, are a source of social capital, contributing to the overall fabric of connection among people and in turn enhancing the experience of people in a wider circle of association. The most significant source of social capital is the faith community. But even this does not substitute for the diversity and richness of a neighborhood where connection exists between people of all generations who might have little in common beyond shared humanity and a vision for caring community.

THE VOICE OF THE SPIRIT IN NEIGHBORLY CONVERSATION

Our social systems are shored up with rules that help us live together with some semblance of peace and order. We humans have created the laws that provide harmony among us, but there is no legal structure that can require us to love our neighbor. Rather, the voice of the Spirit calls us to love our neighbor. This is not just some vague platitude; it is a call to invite one another across the boundaries that divide us, to seek to understand our differences, and to communicate directly and personally. As cultural norms require less and less of us in terms of our social contract with our neighbors, however, we are less in tune to the spiritual call that takes us beyond our lawful obligations. We rely too much on rules to define how we relate, and then we turn too quickly to an outside agency to handle a dispute. In choosing the easy way out, we become increasingly estranged from the neighbors with whom we might create a spirit of caring and responsibility in our local community.

This is estrangement from our neighbors, but it is also spiritual estrangement, whereby we lose touch with who we are in relationship with the holy purpose that holds our world together and compels us toward a vision of harmony and goodness. Thus it is estrangement from God, or the divine principle as we understand it; and as we fall short of doing our part to create community, it is estrangement from ourselves. We settle for less than what we can be; we divide ourselves from the self we yearn to be—that is, someone who cares about the world and its inhabitants. With little expectation coming from the social structures that define our interaction, our only motivation to move beyond those feeble social expectations is an inner longing for the sense of wholeness that comes only with a deep level of commitment, among neighbors, to care for one another and get along together.

Loving our neighbors may be the easy part. It's living with them that is hard.

Loving our neighbors may be the easy part.
It's living with them that is hard.

CHAPTER FOUR

FEAR ITSELF

I USED TO PICK UP HITCHHIKERS—UNTIL I HEARD ABOUT what happened to Tyler, that is. Tyler was somewhere in the southwestern United States, traveling on the interstate headed for California. It was early June, and the young man with the duffel and a backpack looked like some of the college students Tyler had met previously on his trip. The hitchhiker was clean-cut and had on khaki shorts and a clean white polo shirt. He seemed nice enough as they rode for about fifty miles. Then, after they stopped for gas, he pulled a gun on Tyler and told him to turn off the road. They went about five miles from the interstate, into a remote area that was mostly desert shrubs and outcroppings of large rocks. The rider then told Tyler to get out of the car and take off his clothes, down to his underwear. He took Tyler's money and his watch, then got in the car, and drove away. By the time Tyler was able to get some help (this was in the days before cell phones), the young man had had time to abandon the car in a restaurant parking lot and catch a ride with his next victim.

What I remember most about Tyler's description of his experience is the sense of terror that gripped him as he drove further and further away from the main highway with a revolver aimed at his heart. I know this sort of thing doesn't happen often; I know that most hitchhikers just want to get somewhere; I know that it is just fear that prevents me from stopping. But I also know Tyler, and what happened to him.

So I don't pick up hitchhikers anymore. Come to think of it, I don't see nearly as many people thumbing rides anymore. Whatever trust there was among strangers on the roads probably vanished about the same time the first razorblade was supposedly detected in a Halloween apple, and the drug companies started sealing up analgesic tablets in tamper-proof containers to deter anonymous assassins from contaminating the pills.

THE REAL DANGER

Perhaps it is not wise for me to pick up hitchhikers, but neither do I want fear to determine my behavior toward strangers in need. As I consider the struggle that goes on within me in a situation where I confront the dilemma of helping or ignoring a stranger who appears to be in need, I recall an e-mail correspondence I received from a friend, Jerry Godard, several years ago. In this moving account, he described an experience from the night before on a road near his home:

> On my way home about eleven last night, I came upon a car showing front-end smoke and some flames, with a black teen-age girl waving for help. It being a deserted semi-country road, I followed my recent declaration and admonition to others not to stop alone at night for seeming emergencies, but drive on to make a phone call for assistance (a recent string of muggings, including a murder, in such settings being my motive). After ten seconds of anguish (that seemed more like an hour), I braked and backed up, with an expletive or three. She was black and young, in trouble and in greater danger than I. (Vainly, I supposed that, if it was a setup, I'd run into the woods.) It wasn't a setup. A wiring fire had ignited insulation and the hood latch was so hot, it wouldn't open at first. Except for a second-degree burn the size of silver dollar on the inside of my forearm, and a lost hour and a half, I came out OK. Oh, Sarah, I don't want to live in a world where I leave someone I believe to be in danger, because it might be a danger to me.

Jerry wrote this letter to me many years ago, but his final sentence compresses time with its disarming sting of moral clarity. When I wrote to ask him if I could have his permission to include it in this book, he reflected further on the experience:

Years later, the white scar on my arm remains a marker. My fear of strangers—a potent, inborn human characteristic—was overwhelmed that night in a flash of tacit recognition that the otherness of the stranger is always, already in me and in those I love. That young woman was inseparable from my daughter, or from you, standing alone, frightened, and in trouble on the side of the road at night. In that uncanny moment, I knew her terror and her longing as if they were my own. To drive by without stopping would be to leave a living piece of myself to die.

Again, it was his final sentence that moved me, with its poignant and spiritual affirmation of who he was in relationship to the stranger and who the stranger was to him. The real danger to him was not to his physical life, but rather a quashing of the core of compassion in his spirit.

I am reminded of what happened recently to another friend, Rhonda, who was walking in a park and heard someone call for help from a short distance away. She beckoned to two people on bicycles to join with her in responding to the plea, for surely there would be less danger for three people than for one. They refused, however. So she responded alone, feeling fearful of what she might encounter. The cries of distress came from a ravine below the bike path, where a young woman had apparently slipped and twisted her ankle. Rhonda used her cell phone to call for help and stayed with the young woman until the police arrived.

Rhonda, like Jerry, was afraid. Like Jerry, she listened to the voice of Spirit, the voice of connection, the voice of compassion, because it was louder than the voice of fear.

DON'T TAKE CANDY FROM A STRANGER

Another set of instincts comes into play, however, when it is our children, not ourselves, for whom we fear. This is not based on a perception of danger to ourselves, but rather an urge to protect our kin. Watch what happens to a female dog that has just given birth to a litter. No matter how docile she may be under normal circumstances, she is likely to snap at any creature that comes near her young.

Humans are not much different. My friend Patrick, for example, is a student of human nature and engages easily with strangers. He is even drawn by the inner edge of risk that he feels when he encounters someone who presents a threat, and he enjoys the rush of adrenalin that reminds him he is alive. He also recognizes his own ambivalence regarding this attraction to what is unknown and unpredictable. When his wife became pregnant with their first child, his fascination with strangers was dramatically countered by his male instinct to keep watch over his family. As he puts it, "If anyone comes close to me and mine, the hair goes up on the back of my neck."

Children, of course, are particularly vulnerable. I recently watched a television segment that demonstrated how easy it is for a stranger to abduct a child. Several children were playing in a park as a man approached them and asked if they had seen his dog. Although they had not, they listened attentively and sympathetically as he described his pet. Then he asked them to help him hunt for the dog; the camera followed the man and the children as they went through the park gate and left in search of the animal.

I was appalled to see how easy it was for this man to lure children away from their safe environment. We teach our children not to take candy from a stranger; never, ever should they get into a car with a stranger. Yet here were several children who had been duly warned, all scurrying out of a park calling out the name of a fictitious dog.

Then I realized that there was a subtler and more disturbing effect of this program. There is no fear like that of parents for the safety of their children. The program fed that fear, no doubt to encourage parents to educate their children about the sinister strangers who might snatch them from the sidewalk on their way to school or abduct them as they walk a block to visit a neighbor. The fact is, more children are seriously hurt as a result of accidents or violence in their own homes than by strangers, and most of those young faces we see on milk cartons belong to children who were kidnapped by one of their own parents.

The effect of this kind of TV program may be to instill healthy and appropriate caution; but it can also inspire parents to nurture a general spirit of distrust for strangers. In the effort to protect children from harm, the producers may also be perforating the layer of "thin trust" among strangers that builds a strong community among people. *Thin trust* is a term Robert Putnam uses to describe what we experience with people we do not know personally, as opposed to the "thick trust" applying to our close relationships. Extolling thin trust for its value in building social networks and social capital, Putnam notes the sad dilemma of its having been eroded over the past few decades: "As the social fabric of a community becomes more threadbare, . . . its power to undergird norms of honesty, generalized reciprocity and thin trust is enfeebled."[1]

TO BECOME LIKE A CHILD

Children go through a period early in life, perhaps around the age of thirteen months or so, when they are instinctively afraid of strangers. This is disconcerting to grandparents, for example, trying to hold their own grandchild but having to hand the screaming child back to a parent. The child's response is not a rejection of any particular individual. The fear is part of the innate and mysterious survival apparatus that equips all creatures for confronting the hazards of living, and the child's impulse to stay near a parent protects it at a vulnerable point.

Once children move through this stage, however, they develop a trust that distinguishes their childlike way of interacting with others. Marta Flanagan captures the quality of holy intimacy that children make possible in her description of an encounter she had with a four-year-old child in a restaurant:

I met Seth in a cheap Mexican restaurant. The night before a professional conference was to begin I sat alone at a table in Hot Springs, Arkansas. It was me, two cheese enchiladas, and a novel I had begun on the plane. From around the corner up a few steps to a mezzanine area in the restaurant, peered a child. I could feel his stare. I turned toward him. "Hi," he said.

"Hi," I said.

"I'm Seth. What's your name?"

"Marta."

He was a boy with straight blonde hair cut like a bowl around his face. "How old are you, Seth?"

"I'm going to be four," he said.

I took a bite of my enchilada. "Are you here with your Mom?" I asked.

"Yes. We came with my grandmother."

I said, "I bet they're talking and drinking coffee right now."

Seth said, "Yeah, and smoking cigarettes." I smiled.

"Where do you live?" Seth asked.

"In a place called Boston," I said. "Tonight I have to sleep in a strange room, in a strange bed in a hotel. How do you feel about sleeping in a bed that isn't your own?"

Seth looked down and said, "It's easier with a night-light." I agreed. It is easier with a night-light.

A mother's voice called to Seth and Seth disappeared. Then he was back.

"Are you a stranger?" he asked.

"Yes, I am a stranger," I said.

"But I know who you are," he said. "You're Marta."

"Yes," I said. "But I'm still a stranger. Seth, you are a stranger to me." He shook his head in disbelief. He couldn't imagine himself as a stranger.

Ah, to be a week short of your fourth birthday, to know the darkness of a strange room and the comforts of a night-light, to approach the stranger with a curious and caring heart—the purity of it fills me with longing. There are those who would say I am wiser than the four-year-old. I would say I simply carry more baggage.

Like Marta, I long for the curious and caring heart that defined the quality of her interaction with Seth. The child's trust and openness are part of the unconscious (and unself-conscious) years of innocence. Those years come to an end for most children somewhere around the age of seven, as they spend more time away from the watchful eyes of adults. It becomes necessary for them to shed some of their innocent trust and move more warily in the world of strangers.

The loss of the young child's kind of trust, although a normal phase of human development, is a facet of the separation of the individual self from the divine Self. When Jesus said that one must become like a child to enter God's domain, I hear him saying that our reunion with Spirit depends on our being able to redeem the quality of trust that only a child seems to possess. Children are able to receive without reservation, and give without judgment. A child sees through eyes undimmed by cynicism and hears with ears unpolluted by too much information. A child's trust is pure—an offering of divine love in our midst.

"Are you a stranger?" Seth asked Marta. Yes, she answered, adding, *"Seth, you are a stranger to me."* I can picture the incredulity in Seth's eyes at the thought that he was himself a stranger to anyone. To redeem the child's perspective is not only to eclipse the strangeness of another person in a few minutes, but also to be startled at the thought that you are a stranger to her, or anyone else.

Redemption into a child's way of trusting is actually a thick (enduring and committed) trust that makes thin trust possible. This kind of trust has a spiritual component, as it invites us to transcend fear and self-centeredness and takes us beyond the tribal familiarity that characterizes most of the trust we nurture in our personal relationships. Our trust is not so much of the other person as it is an expression of faith in the spiritual power that binds us to one another. It is dependent less on the behavior of those people "out there" than it is on how we anchor our trust in the Spirit. We evolve out of the child's innocence into adult experience, then, in faith, to what poet William Blake called a *higher* innocence. If in innocence we are too naïve, and in experience too cynical, then a higher innocence moves toward a trust that, though alert, also extends the self in trust in spite of what we know; it strives toward the child's kind of trust. This is not an invitation to be foolhardy; it is a call to nurture trust as a value, thus cultivating more trustworthiness in others as well.

To cling to one's own kin and friends is a natural, instinctive part of human experience. It is where we learn the thick trust that binds us to our closest companions. But to stay in this clannish circle creates a condition that threatens not only us as individuals but also our whole species. If there is a Darwinian survival principle at work in our earliest fear instincts, there is also such a principle at work in our impulse to develop a network of trust among strangers. To weaken this thin trust places an undue burden upon the trust in our close, intimate bonds; that is, it creates an expectation that our smaller circle of family and friends provides a safe environment for us. Like the security gates and alarms that we install to protect our home or housing development, this tribal turning inward creates a wall between people outside the clan and us.

In fact, if to nourish our significant relationships we rely on thick trust to the exclusion of thin trust, both our relationships and our own core of being are diminished, for they lack the strand of spiritual linkage that is their true strength. I have known couples and families who are so closely knit that they do not even need many friends. They find completeness in one another. There is no question of their genuine love or their trust, but they also become dependent on their bond to the point that when one of them dies, the survivor is *in*complete. The grief is not just the loss of a beloved companion; it is the loss of self.

To a certain extent, of course, this is an unavoidable part of what it means to love, particularly when our loving becomes a commitment through many years of living together. But we should not be so fully completed by our love with one person that we are incomplete without that person. When the trust becomes so thickly enmeshed in one relationship that it severs connection elsewhere, then it becomes unhealthy and endangered. A healthy bond requires that we dilute this trust by expanding our circle of trusting relationships. At the same time, our closer ties solidify the trust we want to build among strangers and others who are part of our larger circle of association.

Curiously, it is the thin trust of the bond with strangers that dilutes the thick trust of a primary relationship to a level that empowers loving and giving within our most committed relationships. For those of us who seek a spiritual dimension in our relationships, our smaller circle of love and trust then becomes a font of blessing to the world; what we receive in turn from the world of interdependent connections lessens the fear factor in our close relationships. To feel our connection with the larger community, after all, is to befriend strangeness and render it less threatening. There is not only a ripple effect but a mutual and enriching exchange of the kind of trust that builds more trust; ripples meet and merge to create a dynamic much larger than any of us who participate in it.

THE COLOR OF FEAR

Another aspect of fear of the stranger that cannot be overlooked is the color or culture factor. Although Chapter Five explores dimensions of racial or cultural difference that affect how we encounter many strangers, this topic also belongs here. When Jerry Godard related his fear of stopping to help the young woman who was stranded on the road late at night, he was conscious that he was white and she was black. He was also a strong male athlete, at least three times her age. Something entirely nonrational was at play in the reaction of this man who had walked with black women and men from the ball field at Brown's Chapel to the Edmund Pettus Bridge in Selma, Alabama, on March 7, 1967. Perhaps it was because of his commitment to antiracism and his loathing for the prejudice in his own heart that he was so sensitive to the moment of hesitation, the moment when he wondered if this was a setup, the moment when he thought of driving past the young woman whose disabled car was spewing smoke into his path.

He did not only hesitate; given his history, he felt guilty for hesitating. The fear buried in his nature became conscious, and thus less likely to influence his actions.

Usually I hear stories about this kind of racial dynamic from the perspective of my African American friends, rather than that of my white companions. Nelson, for example, is a university professor. He describes an occasion when he was speaking at a conference in a large midwestern city. Returning to his hotel, dressed in his Brooks Brothers suit and carrying his laptop computer in a black leather bag, he was walking at a brisk pace behind three white women. It was about dusk. When they spotted him, they immediately consulted with one another in furtive whispers; then they quickened their pace and turned into a restaurant.

This was not the first time he sensed that someone was afraid of him, for no other apparent reason than that he was black and they were white. In an episode similar to Jerry's, Nelson had also stopped to help a young white woman whose car had broken down. When she saw him coming, the woman got inside the car and locked the doors and told him that help was on the way, thank you very much.

Although Nelson is angered by incidents such as these, he is philosophical about it and tends not to take it personally. "It's more about them than about me," he says. Personal or not, however, these encounters affect his relationships with many of his white friends and companions.

IN THE UNFRIENDLY SKIES OF TERROR

With a large-scale disaster such as the terrorist attacks of September 11, 2001, fear of the stranger can turn into panic; subtle expressions of racial prejudice can become a widespread infection of xenophobia. After September 11, paranoia was particularly palpable in the so-called friendly skies, which were violated as never before when Islamic radicals breached airport security, hijacked four airplanes, and flew them on a mission of death. People in the United States and abroad canceled plans for air travel, and airlines scaled back scheduled flights in an effort to compensate for lost revenue. Members of the National Guard were posted in airports, and security agents flew undercover on selected flights. The way to address the American malaise of fear, it seemed, was to make a show of tightened security.

Although I certainly support measures that can reduce the risks of terror in the sky and elsewhere, I think much of this effort was saber rattling for the benefit of panicked citizens rather than a genuine deterrent to terrorists. I don't believe legislation or any detection devices addresses the real problem—not unless we can legislate against hatred and detect the wound deep in the heart of a righteous fanatic. As for the effectiveness of airport security, I heard someone sum it up when he said that increasing security measures against terrorists was something like a giant trying to swat a flea. Learn to detect metal, and terrorists make bombs of plastic; learn to detect plastic, and they will use wax. Confiscate pocketknives, and they will use a broken bottle or a box of matches. And so on. If we put our faith in legislation or technology, we are putting our faith in fear itself. If we expect government to get control of the problem, then we invite government to get control of us. John Adams once said that "fear is the foundation of most governments."[2] It is most assuredly the foundation of oppressive government. Even Adolf Hitler admitted that the one combination weapon most effective against human reason is "terror and force."[3]

Franklin D. Roosevelt was surely right when, in delivering his inaugural speech in 1933, he addressed the depression panic that was gripping the nation by saying "the only thing we have to fear is fear itself—nameless, unreasoning, unjustified terror which paralyzes needed efforts to convert retreat into advance."[4] The president was echoing the words of Henry David Thoreau: "Nothing is so much to be feared as fear."[5] Both of them in turn reflect wisdom from Proverbs: "Do not be afraid of sudden panic, or of the ruin of the wicked. . . ."[6]

Suppressing fear, however, isn't just a matter of willing it away, particularly when you live with terrorism or the threat of it. After the September 11 attacks, columnist Bob Herbert wrote about the effect of fear on the people of New York: "Terror has wormed its way into our daily routine. A sense of dread hovers over the city, undermining the most ordinary activities. Some New Yorkers are afraid to ascend to the upper floors of tall buildings. Others are reluctant to go down into the subways." A cab driver taking Herbert to work said he used to enjoy going to the airport. "Now I see the airport as a source of trouble. Not only that. I don't like driving in tunnels anymore. Or over bridges. I can imagine one of these bridges going splash into the water. These are not good feelings for someone in my profession." In New York, wrote Herbert, people lead two lives. While going about their normal routines, they also have another life that has been dealt to them by the terrorists: "It affects most New Yorkers and consists primarily of a heightened sense of caution, varying degrees of anxiety and fear, and a sharply etched sense of grief for the thousands lost on September 11 and the wounds inflicted on the city as a whole." Then he added, "We'll be leading this dual, disorienting existence for some time."[7]

Living with this kind of fear not only affects every person's individual life, but also has a malignant effect on a democratic social system. David Grossman, an Israeli who has lived his whole life in the shadow of terrorism, wrote about what happens to your psyche in a moving piece that appeared several years ago in the *Los Angeles Times*. He describes a way of life in which citizens are surrounded by their protectors—guards at every corner, alarm buttons in schools, searches and roadblocks, phone taps, secret arrests. A typical excuse for an act of violence is to say, "I thought he was a terrorist." Living with terrorism changes us in ways we barely perceive. We lose much of our humanity and without intentionally doing so, we start categorizing people by their ethnic traits. Grossman identifies the subtle effects of fear on one's consciousness: Terror, he writes, "quickly returns people to a violent, pugnacious, murderous and chaotic 'natural state.'" Noting the effects of terrorism on his own country, Grossman observes that the price people pay for a high level of security is their humanity and the hardening of the soul.

Terrorism, says Grossman, "is frightening in its simplicity: In order to have a democratic, serene and safe way of life, we need the goodwill of nearly all our citizens." That, he explains, is both the secret and the weakest point . . . of democracy: "All of us are, when it comes down to it, each other's hostages."[8]

All of us are, when it comes down to it, each other's hostages. Indeed, once we understand what this means, then we can grasp how urgent is our need to disarm the fear that holds us captive.

Whether we are afraid to board an airplane or worried about being mugged on the subway, fear of the stranger becomes particularly insidious when we think we have to arm ourselves against the threat of violent attack. It is a distinctively American dis-ease that has led to increased use of violent measures to protect against violence.

This is the point at which fear of the stranger becomes mostly a function of human imagination gone amok. Criminals prey on fear. The more fearful you are, the more power they have. When you buy a weapon to protect yourself from them, you have given them yet more power, for they have planted the seed of violence in you. Whether a gun is in the hands of a thief or in the drawer of your nightstand, it is still an instrument of violence. I've been told that having a gun in your home makes it five times more likely that someone in your household will commit suicide, and three times more likely that someone will be murdered.

The spiritual power that Martin Luther King Jr. garnered to inspire the civil rights movement in the United States was *soul force,* the same nonviolent method of response that Mahatma Gandhi called *ahimsa* and used to dismantle institutionalized racism in India. At the core of their teachings was one pure and vital principle, common to their Christian and Hindu faiths: do not return violence with violence. King admonished that we should never allow any enemies to pull us so low as to hate them. Although terrorism introduces dimensions of evil that challenge these principles as never before, the foundational spiritual teaching calls us to resist feeling hate or employing violence to address violence.

Fear is a normal, healthy human response, an essential survival mechanism; but it also has deadly and destructive potential. It can teach you reasonable caution—but it can create a wall of prejudice and distrust between you and others. It can alert you to danger, or provoke you to engage in violent behavior. It can spur you to inform your children wisely, and it can cause you to frighten them unnecessarily. Fear can open your heart to your human vulnerability, or it can imprison you inside of yourself. If you allow yourself to become a hostage to fear—to be pulled so low as to hate or become violent—you give power to the fearmongers; you concede your integrity to that minority of people whose violent behavior terrorizes your heart and cuts you off from the resources of human community.

The only thing I know to do with fear is name it. Disarm it. Name what you feel it doing to you. Name what freedoms it takes away from you. Look it in the face and stare it down, learning to distinguish between a discerning alertness and unreasoning terror. By disarming the fear within yourself, and befriending it as a natural and instinctive mechanism, you learn to live with it and use it rather than being used by it.

The first time I boarded an airplane after the September 11 hijackings was an occasion for staring down fear. Even before the increased threat of terrorism, I was fearful about flying; it means putting my life in the hands of pilots and mechanics and equipment and weather—all of which I have no ability to control. Although I have always received a certain thrill from looking down at the earth from thirty thousand feet, I also tend to recall every fluky airplane disaster that has occurred in my adult life. If I am sitting in the back of the plane, I recall a DC10 that had the rear engine blow out; if I am near the front, I remember the big hole in the front of a plane out of Hawaii. This is not a huge fear or panic, but it is the kind of fear that could, if allowed to take hold, prevent me from flying at all. Before I fly I ask myself, *Is this trip worth risking my life for?* Generally the answer is no, but there I am, because if I didn't get on the plane, I would be giving in to the fear; I would be its hostage. I would give up the freedom to travel long distances in a matter of hours. Along with that freedom, other freedoms would be eroded as well.

Boarding my flight for Seattle a month after the attacks, I felt uneasy. But then, so did many others, and I suspected I was not the only one asking myself if this trip was worth risking my life for. I was also not the only one sizing up fellow passengers for their potential as wielders of violence. In a curious way, the knowledge that I was probably not alone in my fear had its own disarming effect. Exchanging knowing smiles with other passengers, I sensed that we took our seats with a deepened awareness that, although alone in our personal struggles with fear, we were all in this together.

Fear of the stranger is not always fear of harm, however. Sometimes it is combined with an attraction such as Patrick described when he admitted his ambivalence; what we fear is that we may be lured out of our comfort zone and into an encounter that will challenge us, change us, or require us to make a commitment. Someone told me recently that he enjoyed interacting with strangers because he didn't owe them anything and he could walk away from them, free of obligation. He is wrong, of course. Yes, you can walk away. But if you have been touched by the interaction, you take something from it with you.

One of my favorite stories of what it means to be touched by the power of the Spirit in such an interaction is from the biblical book of Genesis. Jacob was on his way to meet his twin brother, Esau, at a time when the brothers had not seen each other for twenty years—not since Jacob had bought Esau's birthright and then stolen their father's final blessing from him. Jacob had fled when he heard that Esau planned to kill him. But now, many years later, Esau invited Jacob to return and was on his way out (with his household and an army of four hundred men) to meet him.

Jacob's heart was full of fear and hope as he set out with his family and all of their animals, servants, and possessions to return home. Perhaps Esau had set a trap and was planning to ambush them all. On the eve of their rendezvous, Jacob sent the others in his party ahead, across the river Jabbok, and he stopped to camp on the river's edge alone.

There, throughout the night, Jacob wrestled with a stranger. Pinned in Jacob's throttlehold, the stranger touched Jacob's thigh and put it out of joint, and begged to be released before the sun rose. Jacob demanded a blessing. The stranger gave him a new name, *Israel,* as a recognition that he had striven with God and with men and had prevailed. Then he blessed Jacob. Jacob named the place where they had struggled *Peni'el* (meaning "the face of God"), saying, "For I have seen God face to face, and yet my life is preserved." Jacob then limped away, changed forever by the encounter.[9]

Jacob went on to meet Esau, who embraced him, fell on his neck, and kissed him. They wept together in a poignant and moving scene of reconciliation.

There are many levels of interpretation for this story and the impact of Jacob's encounter. In its most particular and personal application, it is a story of a man who stopped at a river crossing and felt the full brunt of his own fear come in upon him. During the night, he struggled with a stranger. He was both injured and blessed by his encounter with the stranger; it was, in fact, an encounter with God.

CHAPTER FIVE

THERE BUT FOR THE GRACE OF GOD . . .

SOME YEARS AGO, I ATTENDED A CONFERENCE HELD ON the campus of Yale University in New Haven, Connecticut. Yale is located downtown, and it was my custom to get out of the hotel or university setting for most of my meals. One morning, as I was in town looking for a place to have breakfast, an African American man approached me and said, "I'm staying in the shelter and I haven't had anything to eat for a long time. I'm very hungry. Could you give me enough money for something to eat? I promise you I'm not on drugs or alcohol; I just need some money for food." He repeated his request, and his assurance that he was drug-free, a few times before pausing to let me respond. I suspect he was quite accustomed to being rebuffed.

"I don't want to give you money," I told him, "but I am on my way to breakfast now, and I'll buy you something to eat. What do you want?" I had made similar offers in the past to people who asked for money in the city streets, and no one had ever accepted my invitation. This man must have truly been very hungry. He was not particular, so we found a small café and took our seats at the counter. The breakfast crowd had thinned out, so it was not very busy.

For about ten minutes we sat there, first looking over the menu, then chatting. I learned that his daughter had just graduated from high school and was enrolled in college for the fall. He had missed the graduation ceremony but was very proud of her.

During this time, the waitress passed in front of us back and forth between the coffee pot and the customers in booths. We were not even offered coffee. I began to get irritated as the waitress poured coffee and took orders for a couple of people who came in after we did.

I spoke politely to her, saying, "We would like to have some coffee and place our order, please."

"I'm very busy," she snapped. "I'll get to you as soon as I can."

Several more minutes elapsed before I finally began to catch on: we were not going to be served. I went to the cash register, where there was a man who looked as if he might be a manager, and explained to him that we were not being waited on. Without apologizing, he came over and took our order himself.

I learned more about discrimination in those ten minutes of being ignored at that counter than at any other time in my entire life.

My companion had no bitter words. He was grateful to get a meal. He told me he enjoyed talking with me. I was disturbed, however, by something in his manner. It is difficult to describe, but I was reminded of the feeling one has when a noble animal has had the passion in its nature tamed out of it. Even his gratitude demeaned him, and his countenance spoke to me of another level of humiliation, one in which I, the charitable person who responded to his hunger, participated unintentionally and unknowingly. As we parted, I felt a sense of sadness and unease, even with the role I had played in the lunch counter drama.

HEAVEN IS A POTLUCK PARTY

Sitting at a table where we share a meal together is one of the most common experiences we have with other people, mostly people we know. It is also one of the most discriminating, in the sense that how we choose the people with whom we eat is a universal gauge of our comfort or discomfort with people who are not like us. Perhaps that is why many of the parables of Jesus, written in ancient times and relevant in the third millennium, focus on situations where people eat together.

One such parable is the one about the feast. In *The Essential Jesus,* John Dominic Crossan offers a version based on the Gospel of Thomas (64:1–11):

A host sent his servant to invite friends to an impromptu
    dinner party

He said to the first: "My master invites you this evening"
The first replied: "I must wait for merchants who owe me money
Please excuse me"

He said to the second: "My master invites you this evening"
The second replied: "I must arrange my friend's wedding
    banquet
Please excuse me"

He said to the third: "My master invites you this evening"
The third replied: "I must collect the rent from a new estate
Please excuse me"

The servant reported that all had excused themselves and the
    host said
"Go out to the streets
and bring in to my dinner party
anyone you happen to find"[1]

Crossan's narrative suggests that the dinner party in God's domain is a rather potluck affair—meaning not the food but the guests, who are a diverse lot of strangers indiscriminately invited. In particular, this potluck event brought together the somebodies and the nobodies who would otherwise never have associated with one another.

In his version of the familiar text from the sermon on the mount about how the first will be last and the last will be first, Crossan further describes the spiritual logic of Jesus in terms of the somebodies and the nobodies:

> The somebodies will be nobodies
> and
> the nobodies will be somebodies[2]

In the homes and villages of Galilee, children were among the people who did not have power. They were nobodies, especially female children. An infant was a nobody unless its father accepted it as a member of the family. A father, then, could direct a mother to dump a baby—usually a girl—into the garbage or give the infant to someone to be raised as a slave. Other nobodies included women, slaves, and peasants. It was absolutely unthinkable for the somebodies and the nobodies to sit down to share a meal.

So when Jesus told this parable about a somebody inviting strange nobodies to come into his house for a meal, he was suggesting something quite revolutionary. A man decides to give a dinner party, but none of his friends can come. So, bringing in anyone off the streets, he may have men sitting next to women, children with adults, free next to slave, socially high next to socially low, and ritually pure next to ritually impure. All the boundaries that keep people safely within their social identities are shattered.

This was Jesus' notion of the kingdom of God. The nobodies become somebodies and the somebodies become nobodies. That is, you don't distinguish which is which.

To make things worse, of course, he didn't just tell stories; he *practiced* this egalitarian approach. He actually ate and drank with people who were a serious threat to his reputation. We all know about guilt by association, right? Hang around with criminals, and you are labeled a criminal. Hang around with prostitutes, and people assume you are a paying customer or a colleague. Well, this is what it amounted to. Jesus lived in a place and time where any unmarried woman who was in a social situation outside male control was considered a woman of ill repute.

So Jesus was accused of being a glutton and a drunkard, of hanging out with prostitutes and other outcasts or untouchables. He defied the social code, turned things upside down. In most of the developed world, we don't really have a context for understanding how revolutionary this was because we do not have codes that forbid one group of people from associating with another. We are not so very many years, however, from the time when Jewish people in Europe had to wear yellow armbands or stars sewn to their clothing, or the time when dark-skinned people could not eat in many restaurants in the southern United States. In many parts of the world, women are still nobodies. Girl babies in China are still being discarded or abandoned and left to die. The caste system in India may be illegal, but in 2002 some parents still murder their children when a lower-caste Juliet dares to consort with a higher-caste Romeo.

If you think we Westerners are without our social boundaries, go out and pick up one of your city's street people. Take the person not to a counter in a café but to a five-star restaurant for dinner. Watch how people react.

It isn't done.

It is, however, what Jesus did, and at the core of the radical egalitarianism that was the essence of his spiritual teaching.

His was not an example of charitable giving, but of shared living. Although I cannot claim to walk the same path as Jesus, my experience of working with shelters, soup kitchens, and food pantries has acquainted me with a dynamic that we often unknowingly generate with our charitable activity. It is generally comfortable, in these settings, to be in a serving role. For example, when I visited a shelter for homeless men to serve them a meal, I enjoyed setting the table or serving the food. This was part of our church's outreach in the community.

Then we decided to invite the men from the shelter for a potluck meal at the church, where they would sit at the table with members of the congregation. Instead of ladling soup, I was among those served. Although there was still no question that we were the hosts and they were the guests, the social constellation was changed; I did not have a servant role to further insulate me or set me apart from the guests. It was when we were seated together for a meal that I had an opportunity to become acquainted with the men at the shelter as individuals with names, families, occupations, hobbies, and opinions. It was then that I realized the threat of their strangeness was not so much in the fact they were homeless as it was in the artificial separation created by the roles we assumed because of the circumstances. When one of the shelter residents began to attend Sunday services and volunteered to help with the fall bazaar, the distinction of roles dissolved.

GRACE HAPPENS

Some people might say of those they serve at the soup kitchen, "There but for the grace of God go I." I think what they really mean is, "There *by* the grace of God *am* I," for surely God's grace does not single some of us out for privilege and allow others to suffer. Divine grace, however, brings us into dialogue with the stranger at the table and the stranger within; it acquaints us with the part of ourselves that is reflected in someone who is, by our definition anyway, deemed less fortunate.

At no time have I felt this brand of grace more poignantly than the day I walked downtown and saw a woman wearing my red dress.

The tailored red dress with a double-breasted bodice, straight skirt, and matching belt was a favorite, but it was two sizes too large for me. Still, I clung to it for several years after losing some weight. Then I realized that keeping the dress meant I planned to regain the unwanted pounds. With that awareness I decided to give it to the local shelter.

The woman in my red dress gazed toward me but appeared not to see me. Her long, wispy hair was uncombed and tangled into a lumpy knot at the crown of her head. The dress, which I had donated thinking that perhaps someone could wear it to interview for a job, hung loosely on her skeletal frame; it was wrinkled, torn, and askew. She was not on her way to an interview, to be sure.

Yes, it was a moment of grace, that vision of rumpled red. There, by the grace of God, I saw myself.

Our epiphanies of holy intimacy are a glimpse of the strangeness or the fear of strangeness in ourselves. What I registered in my psyche that day was knowledge of what can become of us, even those of us who have grown up in a world of privilege. When I worked at a shelter that served mostly women and children, I was amazed at how many of the guests were, in fact, not much different from me. Having known times of being on the edge financially, I understand what it means to be one paycheck away from eviction. Having lived with family members who were mentally ill or alcoholic, I am no stranger to the twists of circumstance that can land a person in the streets. Illness, unemployment, addiction, disability: Whose life has not been touched by at least one of these? Who, indeed, might we be if circumstances render us devastated by misfortune?

To see ourselves in a stranger is to see something that we may not even be aware is there. We shed our clothes as a snake molts its skin, and move on to another stage of our lives. I have been taken aback on other occasions when I saw my clothing on people I knew—usually people who shopped at the church rummage sale. Even then, when I knew the person, it was as if a bit of my past came to visit me. The inner stranger, then, was a self of the past, a person who dressed—and perhaps lived and thought—in a different style.

GUESS WHO'S COMING TO DINNER?

We do not always recognize the grace or power of the mirror that is held up for us by a stranger, at least not in the hour of revelation. Such was the case for Louise and Justin, whose lives were touched and transformed over a period of several years by an unwelcome stranger in their home.

Louise and Justin grew up in Mississippi. Teenage sweethearts, they graduated from their segregated high school in the late 1950s and then went on to attend Old Miss, where James Meredith intruded on their white world of football games and fraternities with his challenge to the university's policy of segregation.

Louise and Justin had never known any "colored people," as they called them then, except Tillie, the maid who worked for Louise's family once a week. But their Baptist upbringing had taught them enough about what was right and wrong for them to be appalled when they witnessed the mobs of people, some of them their own friends, who participated in the riots and demonstrations when Meredith was admitted to the school in 1962. Louise was disgusted by this display of hatred, but she ended up adopting an attitude toward African Americans that was as dehumanizing as that of her bigoted friends. Instead of considering them all inferior, she lumped them together as noble, and oppressed . . . and in need of being saved. She wanted to save them all.

Louise and Justin got married when they graduated from the university; she taught in elementary school while he went to law school. When he took his first job, they had the first of their three children, Holly.

Still living in a largely segregated community in the South, Louise devoted most of her time to raising the children, PTA, the bridge club, tennis, and volunteering for hospice. Justin became a partner in his law firm, and they were able to save money toward college for their children.

Their image of family bliss was shattered, however, when Holly was sixteen. That was when Justin and Louise drove downtown one evening and saw her in front of a movie theater holding hands with her boyfriend, Don. This was their first awareness of Don, and the only thing they noticed about him at the time was the color of his skin: it was a very, very dark brown.

They felt shocked, angry, and betrayed. In addition, they were upset by their own feelings, for they had not expected to react so negatively to seeing their daughter holding hands with a young man of another race. They thought of themselves as open-minded, but this relationship did not fit their "three children, two cats, and a yard" image of family, and they felt devastated by it. Distraught though they were, however, they did not push for Holly to stop seeing Don. They thought her "black phase" would pass; it was just a teenage period of rebellion.

Their family image was permanently altered when, a few years later, Holly became pregnant with Don's child. Marriage was not in their plan, but she resisted the idea of abortion. When Brittany was born, Justin and Louise were presented with a new stranger: their beautiful brown-skinned illegitimate granddaughter. Louise was determined not to feel prejudiced toward her own grandchild, but it was difficult at first to accept Brittany's blackness. Justin told Holly, "I will love this child, but I will not raise her or support her."

Justin has "eaten those words many times" in the five years since Brittany came into his life, and his home. "When you eat crow," he says, "it's not bad with a lot of salt on it."

For Justin and Louise, Brittany's strangeness diminished as they became more acquainted with dimensions of their own prejudice—that is, when they broke through the walls of their own denial and admitted their feelings to themselves. Curiously, it was *claiming* their prejudice rather than trying to dispel it that opened them to being with the strangeness and moving through it.

Louise reflected later on her attitude toward African American strangers. To disabuse herself of her own prejudice, she first had to disabuse herself of her own denial. Difficult as it was, she had to recognize that she did not like this young man, and her dislike had to do with racial or cultural characteristics. He was a jive-talker, a slick dude—not James Meredith. Justin, too, admits that he struggled with falling short of who he thought he was. He wanted to be the magnanimous dad with a liberal outlook, and he tried to act the part; but inside he was revolted and embarrassed by his daughter's behavior.

Both Louise and Justin had to contend with the stranger within themselves as they encountered feelings that conflicted with their values. Through their pain, they met themselves in their granddaughter, who was their family and their blood. In her brown face, they saw their own faces. By the grace of God, they claimed themselves—and her.

COFFEE, TEA, OR NAVIGATION?

Every stranger we meet is an individual person. We know that, of course. But many of them also belong to some group about which we make conscious or unconscious assumptions, all filtered through our lives, our cultural context, and our religious perspective. Some strangers are dark-skinned or female or homosexual, or over sixty. They are tattooed or wear nose rings or dye their hair green. They speak with an accent or walk with an attitude. Often we preserve our assumptions about strangers by "lumping" them into groups, where we continue to keep them at a safe distance from our lives and our tidy—sometimes pejorative, sometimes idealized—notion of who they are.

This came home to me in a rather humbling experience I had several years ago, when I was traveling by air across the United States. It took about fifteen hours to get from the East Coast to the West Coast, thanks to mechanical problems on our airplane. By the time we arrived in Los Angeles, however, I had missed my commuter connection. Fortunately, the airline arranged for a bus to transport passengers who missed the flight. I took my seat, feeling weary from a day of travel. The attractive young woman sitting next to me initiated a conversation. She seemed to have some inside knowledge about the *real* reasons our flight was delayed. She said she worked for the airline, and in my mind I pictured her smiling pleasantly and offering drinks and pillows to passengers. Fortunately, I did not give away my sexist assumption before she told me that she was a pilot. I flushed with embarrassment, anyway. Here I was, a woman minister—someone who had broken into a male-dominated profession and had lived with the subtle discrimination of people who were just not ready for a feminine presence in the pulpit. I thought I was an enlightened feminist; to my horror, I was still in the same category with people who automatically think *he* when you mention making an appointment to see your doctor, attorney, or minister.

Some of my gay and lesbian friends have told me that many homosexuals can be homophobic. So I suppose it follows that a feminist can be sexist.

When our encounters with strangers give us a glimpse of our own strange and shadowy self-disdain, it is a gift. Jacquelyn Shropshire Simms, an African American who coordinates Building Bridges, a program of conversation among people of diverse cultural or racial backgrounds, captures the quality of this gift in a poem describing an experience she had with a stranger when she, a newcomer in her town, attended a street festival. She titles it "Prejudiced—Me? Not Much":

A Bele Chere Festival years ago, 1989—
My husband, my daughter, my mother, me—
    genetically sun kissed all.
Having fun. Exploring this possible new home.
Very hot July day. A cool drink—good idea!

Mmm—A frozen fruit drink. Small paper parasol in it.
Good drink . . . Cold . . . Refreshing . . . Slowly sipped.
The last few sips. The drink gone but enjoyed.
The parasol—pretty. Bright colors, tiny. I wear it in my hair.
More to see. More to eat. Tired now. Let's leave.
Hmm. A single guy—white face, black pants, black shirt,
    black motorcycle helmet.
Does he have on a black jacket, too???
    Stay away. Stay away.
A gust of wind. Parasol swept away—
    toward the guy!
Don't go near him—Hell's Angel.
He stoops to reach parasol. Now what?!?
Parasol inches from *his* hand! Another gust.
    Parasol swept farther. Far away.
He looks at me. *Kindness* in his eyes!
Realization: He wanted to retrieve it for me!
I'm touched. I thank him for his kindness.
His caring—more important than the parasol.
Parasol gone. It's okay. Caring stays. I hope he knows. . . .
He walks forever—chasing parasol.
In his clasp—returned to me. Emotion rises—tears fill my eyes.
A lesson here. How to live it?
    A need for bridges. . . .

Building bridges is not something we can accomplish in a single episode of revelation, and most of us will blunder our way through a number of attempts in the course of trying to heal the wounds of injustice. Karin Tanenholtz writes of an experience she had when she and another woman stood side by side at the curb poised to step into a crosswalk:

> We waited for the light to signal us to move along. This wasn't a beautiful day. No sun, and a seemingly never-ending winter. Streets and sidewalks everywhere were filled with slush from a late-night, late-season snow. The thick slush lay unplowed and dirty from traffic. Snowplows seem not to respond very quickly in March, so getting to places in the city was a challenge. I looked over at the woman, who seemed to be surveying the sloppy morass ahead. Her strong brown hands gripped the handle of her baby's stroller.
>
> Just then the crossing signal showed "Go" and I said, "Here, let me help you."
>
> "No!" she retorted. "No one has helped me before and I don't need your help now."
>
> I, Whitey, got told and it stung.
>
> It was a long time before I recognized the grace in that wintry moment. The brief encounter happened many years ago but it planted an understanding of racism's deadly back and forth game. The game will continue until its root-suffering cry is heard.

Karin's experience reminds me of a time when I rushed to open a door for a blind man and he angrily scolded me. Since then, I ask first whether or not people who appear to need help really want any. Often they do, and they accept with gratitude. Even the angry responses that Karin and I experienced from the young mother and the blind man may have been due to what our gestures evoked from their personal history rather than being a reaction to our attempts to be helpful.

Sometimes the desire to lend a hand becomes more barrier than bridge, particularly if it functions as the same kind of insulation that we may have when we ladle soup or donate clothing. It offers a safe and structured venue for our compassionate giving. We want to feel good about ourselves, but we prefer to keep a clear boundary between the helper and those who need help. Without intending to, we participate in a hierarchy of givers and receivers. Reflecting on this, I have a better understanding of what was going on one day when I worked at a soup kitchen. After having abandoned the ever-comfortable ladle to take my place at one of the tables in the social hall at the Episcopal Church, I engaged in conversation with a man who, at the end of our meal, told me he had something he wanted to give me. He disappeared for a few minutes and then returned with a small plastic bottle of hand lotion. *How silly,* I thought at the time, but I put the little blue bottle of lotion in my car—and frequently had occasion to use it. Each time I did, I remembered the man at the soup kitchen. I suspect he just wanted to be on the giving end of the relationship for a change.

THINK AGAIN!

As I review the examples offered in this chapter, I observe a pattern that was not intentional as I began to write. The element of personal revelation experienced in connection with the strangers of these incidents is less about understanding them and more about getting to know ourselves, as a result of the encounters we have with them.

I recall visiting the Simon Wiesenthal Museum of Tolerance in Los Angeles several years ago. The exhibit, which chronicles the horrors of the Nazi Holocaust, gives visitors more than an education. It is an invitation into the most evil dimensions of the human soul. Lest you think you are there as an innocent witness to it all, you begin with the choice of entering the museum through one of two doors. One is marked with the word "prejudiced," and the other reads "unprejudiced." If you attempt to step through the latter portal, you discover that it is locked. In addition, a sign illuminates, flashing its message at you, "Think again!" The only way into the museum is to take a route through the shadow-lined corridor of your own soul.

Strangers who bear the mark of a racial or cultural distinction often invite us to think again, and then to open the door into our own minds and hearts, where we discover some of the barriers that have gradually taken hold there. The invitation may be in an abrupt burst of anger, or in an act of kindness; it may be over a meal shared in a church hall or a café. To accept it and walk through the door may be about as much fun as a tour through a holocaust exhibit. But we do not emerge from our experience the same as when we went in.

CHAPTER SIX

SECRETS AND STRANGERS

A YOUNG MAN WAS TRAVELING ALONE IN THE WHITE Mountains of New England. As dusk darkened the September sky and the wind howled through the pass known as "the Notch," he was drawn to a cottage, where a family gathered around a roaring fire. At their kind invitation to take respite from the chill, he joined them at the hearth.

The conversation that ensued between the stranger and the family is related by Nathaniel Hawthorne in his tale of "The Ambitious Guest."[1] The traveler was a solitary sort, who, "with the lofty caution of his nature," had "kept himself apart from those who might otherwise have been his companions." Likewise the family, "though so kind and hospitable, had that consciousness of unity among themselves and separation from the world at large, which, in every domestic circle, should still keep a holy place where no stranger may intrude."

But some mysterious circumstance on this particular evening drew them into a bond of confidence. As they assembled around the fire, the guest was moved to tell this family of his secret ambition, which was that he wanted to be remembered after his death. With this confidence offered to them, one by one the adult members of the family shared their secret ambitions as well, revealing aspirations they had never before shared even with one another. Connected in what Hawthorne calls "the kindred of a common fate," the family members and their guest spoke of things they wished to accomplish before they died.

They could not know that none of them would realize their dream. Their conversation ended abruptly when they heard the sounds of snow breaking away in the Notch. They ran from the cottage and took refuge in a shelter that had been designed to protect them from the threat of avalanche. Sadly, it was the shelter, not the cottage, that was buried under the frozen deluge. At the end of the story, Hawthorne leaves his readers with the image of the cottage, still standing, with the fire smoldering on the hearth and empty chairs set in a circle around it. The safe refuge, it turned out, had become their tomb, while the momentary circle of vulnerability they had created around the fire survived fully intact.

Hawthorne's cruel irony crushes the hopes of these people under a runaway remnant of winter snow. The story seems to be reminding us that we who would save our lives will lose them.

As a reader of this tale, I receive a glimpse into the warm hearth where the members of a cohesive and self-contained family unit allowed themselves to be touched by a stranger's gift of intimacy and then broke through their own routine way of being with one another to share secret longings. As the smoke from the smoldering fire stole up the mountainside in the silent dawn the next day, ebbing embers of the night's communion, something of their human bond persisted beyond the individuals and their personal ambition.

THE POWER OF CONFESSION

Hawthorne's tale points to a phenomenon that occurs between strangers in many circumstances, not just those where the players share "the kindred of a common fate." Sometimes people are moved to tell secrets, confess failures, or reveal fears to a stranger, even though they have not spoken of these matters with a close companion. The stranger, perhaps not even introduced by name, becomes like a priest hearing confession, but in an objective and uncommitted role that reserves judgment. The stranger may not even offer sympathy or acceptance; what he or she offers is neutrality and anonymity. Unlike a counselor, the stranger does not charge by the fifty-minute hour and is not obliged to respond in any way. Unlike a priest, the stranger does not have authority to offer divine judgment or absolution. Similar to both counselor and cleric, however, the stranger is entrusted with confidential or sensitive personal information.

In the context of a bond that requires neither response nor obligation, a confession becomes a kind of conversation with your own soul.

To speak your secret pain, for example, into the open air between yourself and a stranger is to name it, and name what power it has in your life. From this kind of confession emerges the possibility of defusing the destructive aspects of shame, embarrassment, or guilt. Beyond that, it is a general offering of trust extended to an unknown recipient, perhaps on the basis of intuition. Such trust, whether reciprocated or not, strengthens the human bonds that enable all of us to affirm our human connection with one another, even though it is given and received in virtual anonymity. Although there is no obligation, there is an element of commitment whereby the stranger receives the gift of trust.

It is probably not unusual for a conversation of this nature to take place while people are traveling—particularly on an airplane, where the clearly defined time limit imposed on the encounter can be the kind of structured container in which passengers may respond to one another with unique freedom. My friend Jere Jacob describes an in-flight experience that impressed itself on her memory:

> Some years ago when I was spending the bulk of my time on airplanes in the pursuit of my work in television production, I had as a seatmate on a transatlantic flight a young man who was in apparent distress. Normally, I am one of those people who put on a bland face when in transit in hopes that no one will find occasion to attempt communication beyond anything involving the rearrangement of bodies to ease getting to and from the lavatory. However, on this day, the young man in question was very

agitated, and it was obvious to me that he wished (nay, needed) to talk to someone and that it did not matter too much who that someone might be. Thus, we were in conversation long before the arrival of the peanuts, and this remained the case through the meal, the movie, and the dozing time that normally follows.

This young man was going through a wrenching time of decision in relation to a long-standing relationship that he felt was in jeopardy. He felt betrayed and abandoned by his partner and needed to discern whether or not his perceptions were valid. The virtue of my serving as his sounding board on this occasion as a total stranger is that I had absolutely no investment in him or his partner. I could approach his narrative from a totally unbiased point of view, serve as a true devil's advocate in attempting to find some kind of viable truth, and then serve up to him my "take" on the situation. As our discussion proceeded, he went through a series of processes, all of them very intense and many of them in conflict with one another. He reviewed not only the history they had shared together but also their divergent perceptions of that history. His eyes widened several times during the conversation as he was made aware of the opposing point of view and could examine it dispassionately in the sterile environment we had been provided. I shared confidences with him that I have not trusted to intimate friends and he shared similarly with me. This was, in fact, probably one of the most intense and intimate interactions I have ever had with anyone, including lovers (we all do, after all, hold back a little of our ordinariness from lovers in hopes that they will perpetually find us enchanting).

We parted ways with him having come to a life-changing decision. We first tried shaking hands, then discovered that this was not acceptable and ended up instead in a minutes-long embrace at the luggage carousel. It was a very absorbing trip, and I discovered later that evening as I repaired to my familiar bed that I was emotionally drained.

It never occurred to either of us to ask the other's name, and we had no intention of ever getting in touch again. That would have ruined the interaction we had shared. We were wrapped in the comforting aura of stranger-ness. We could afford to be totally candid with one another, and we could ask anything of one another that this cocoon of time and space allowed. I often think of this young man and wonder if his decision held up in the reality of his world. In a way, I think, it doesn't really matter. What was important that night was that he find methods to confront his demons, to assess his own needs, and to come to a place where he could evaluate and own his feelings. I think he got to that place that night, and I feel deeply privileged to have been present to witness his maturation.

It is a curious phenomenon, this exchange of trust that occurs between strangers. Why is it that we sometimes divulge our secret longing, our deepest wound, or our nagging tug of shame to someone we have never met and know nothing about? I do not really know, but I have observed that it is important that we be able to tell our story to people who are not invested in us, who have no other connection beyond that of the human bond and a common participation in the dynamic of guilt, confession, and forgiveness that functions in settings both sacred and secular.

I think of the old sailor in Samuel Taylor Coleridge's narrative poem "The Rime of the Ancient Mariner," who is compelled by an inner "agony" to tell his story to chosen individuals. Thus it is that he accosts a wedding guest and submits him to his sad tale, recounting how he killed an albatross that flew behind a ship on which he crewed. After he shoots the bird with his bow and arrow, the air goes still, the sea is calm, and the ship stalls. The dead albatross, which is thought to bring the warm winds of good fortune, is hung around the mariner's neck, where it stays as the sailors, one by one, fall dead, cursing him with their eyes. The mariner, all alone, in despair, and unable to die himself, tries to pray, but cannot. Finally, as he watches the slimy water snakes and beholds their beauty, he unconsciously blesses them. The albatross falls off and sinks "like lead into the sea." Once on shore, the mariner seeks out the Hermit in the Wood, so that the Hermit might "shrieve" his soul. When the Hermit entreats him to confess his pain, he is beset with a woeful and wrenching agony, and freed only after his story has been told. From then on, it has been his terrible and exhausting fate to be periodically overcome with the agony, which is not relieved until he tells his ghastly tale.[2]

The principle of confession exercised by the mariner is the same one that brings people together in AA meetings and other twelve-step programs throughout the world to hear and tell their stories. Some tell their stories over and over, as a circle of strangers becomes the agent of the higher power that forgives, blesses, and empowers change. Meanwhile, they too, like the wedding guest who is chosen to hear the mariner's wrenching tale, are changed as well, as their compassion deepens for the pain they receive into their own hearts.

Regardless of our religious beliefs, each of us carries an albatross around our neck—or perhaps a few canaries. It is cleansing and renewing to be able to purge ourselves of our burden, opening the way for forgiveness and change. Sometimes, like the mariner, we accost someone we have never seen. Sometimes we find groups like AA. Many of us would shun the traditional term *repentance,* but our confession is often the first step in a process of contrition and making amends.

IN THE WIDE WORLD OF WEBBING

A growing center for conversation that may lead to confessional offerings and a surprising level of intimacy is the World Wide Web. Strangers can meet twenty-four hours a day on sites where a common interest in something like quilting or fly fishing brings them into conversation, often leading to personal acquaintance, deepening friendship, or life-long commitment. I recently spoke with a woman who was not inclined to use the Web for more than research and information, until she and her husband were struggling with infertility. She needed to talk with others who had suffered with the same problem, but she was a public person, and local support groups were not comfortable for her. She found a supportive network on the Web, where she was assured of privacy and anonymity.

The Web is also a source of connection with the larger human community. At no other time in recent history have I been more drawn to my computer for links of this nature than during the days that followed the terrorist attacks of September 11, 2001. Generally I will delete forwarded messages that appear in my e-mail inbox, and ignore spam. But in those days of shock, terror, and sorrow, I read them all—stories of survivors, commentary by military analysts, and reflections of peace activists. I logged on to the *New York Times* site, eager to feel a daily connection with the suffering city.

A few days before the attack, I renewed acquaintance with Suzie, a high-school classmate whom I located through a newly developed Website. On September 11, our correspondence turned to more personal matters, for her twenty-two-year-old son, who lived in New York, was traumatized. From the Hudson River, in front of the World Trade Center, he watched as a large plane slammed into the Number Two Tower and exploded; he saw people fall or jump from the towers, and minutes later he witnessed the collapse of the pillars of trade and finance that had dominated the skyline of Manhattan. While he was running away, he called from his cell phone and woke his parents in California. Some of his friends were dead—he knew that, for he had worked with them in the building that crumbled before his eyes.

Suzie wanted to know if I had any resources to suggest for him, and she needed support for her own distress. I told her he needed human resources, not books, and gave her some suggestions. I said, "Suzie, you are an important resource, too." Later, she wrote saying, "I don't think he'll feel like returning to his job no matter how much counseling he receives. He can't close his eyes now without seeing people jumping from the tower. He said he'll never fly again and wants us to come get him. My 220 lb. super intelligent son wants his mama and daddy to come pick him up."

It was only a day later that she wrote again to say, "He is unbelievably resilient. Yesterday he was filled with despair and anguish after witnessing the second plane attack and the many who jumped to their death. Today he has anger. I think this is healthy. He is no longer so quick to let terrorists chase him from his job."

I had not seen Suzie for forty years, and we were not close friends in high school, but we wrote daily through the ensuing weeks. Soon we were closing our letters with "Love," or "Much love," naming the bond formed between us. In this capsule of tragedy and vulnerability that brought us into conversation, I shared thoughts with her that I did not share with family and close friends.

How strange it is to think that Suzie and I were there for one another with no other personal link beyond what we had through our computers. Yet this is a daily reality for millions of people who create similar bonds, never knowing one another outside the realm provided by technology.

In addition to the forthright connections that people make on the World Wide Web, multiuser domains (MUDs) have become a popular setting for conversation, including very intimate dialogue. With the technology of the Internet creating its own kind of container, participants in games or chat rooms can log into a cyberconversation at any time of the day or night. They may, in fact, make connections similar to those I have just described, where they use their Web links to carry on a conversation that might also take place over the telephone or in person. Or they may explore another dimension of Webbing, whereby they can wear the mask of anonymity and mine their imagination to create a different kind of experience from what they might have in real life. They do not have to reveal their names. In fact, they do not have to reveal any true statements about themselves.

In effect, those who meet at the cybercafé, the virtual village, or the Web's version of "Dungeons and Dragons," put on a mask, as if they were characters in a theatrical production. Their mode of interaction is reminiscent of the Carnival spirit that occurs every year at Mardi Gras, on Halloween, and in similar festivals all over the world. The Carnival spirit is one of role reversal and masking, and it offers a lens through which we can view some of the masking and role playing that brings people together on the Web.

Mardi Gras, like Carnival in countries that are predominantly Catholic, launches the Christian season of Lent. Suzanne Meyer, a minister who lived at one time in New Orleans, preached to her congregation about the relationship between the wild bacchanalian festival and Lenten restraint: "Carnival and Lent: these seasons are the Yin and the Yang of our lives. As Carnival is a turning outward (literally going out into the streets), a covering up or disguising (masks and costumes), and a time to indulge the flesh, Lent is a turning inward, a time of introspection during which the soul is laid bare, and we restrain those impulses. I think of Carnival and Lent not as representative opposing forces, but as complimentary and necessary opposites in our lives. To fully appreciate the value of one, it is necessary to embrace the other."

Meyer further observed the spiritual function of the Carnival rituals:

For outsiders looking in, Carnival must seem to have all of the charm and appeal of a frat house party: loud music, cheap thrills, casual sex, drunkenness, adolescent humor, stupid rituals, crude parodies of polite society, scantily clad girls, and general bad behavior punctuated occasionally by a guest barfing into the potted plant. It is virtually impossible to convince most outside observers that Carnival is serious business.

Carnival is a phenomenon that immediately challenges our traditional or stereotypical way of making sense out of our world. Like Alice stepping into the Looking Glass, when we step into the world of Carnival everything seems reversed, inverted, and all of the normal rules of understanding no longer apply. At the very least, Carnival has the potential to shake us out of our rigid ways of thinking and thus give us new insight into our existential situation. In this assembly-line world, there are few encouragements to set one's imagination loose.

Carnival reaches virtue not by suppressing our less noble impulses or tightening the reins on what the Jungians would call the shadow side of the human personality, but rather by temporarily liberating the shadow and letting it run free within the boundaries of a carefully constructed public ritual. In Mardi Gras, rather than suppressing our shadows, we are encouraged to set them free for a time once a year in a safe and ritualized setting. An Uptown matron can stroll the venue dressed as a Storyville Madame; a banker can cavort as a pirate or a clown. The most humble worker can wear the raiment of a king. The race, gender, class, or even species to which you were born gives way to your wildest fantasies.

Carnival is primal, holy, and necessary. It is nothing less than a public liturgy, a sacred rite, an outward expression of the collective unconscious. We conceal ourselves in order to reveal ourselves. By masking for Mardi Gras the whole community discloses its true face.

This dynamic of concealing ourselves to reveal ourselves turns up in settings sacred and secular, from the priest's confessional to Bourbon Street. It is interesting to note that Mardi Gras culminates on Shrove Tuesday, the day before Ash Wednesday. The word *shrove* derives from *shrive,* an archaic reference to the confession of one's sins as part of the process of inner purification that is central to all major religious traditions. It is the term used by the ancient mariner when he approaches the Hermit in the Wood with his plea, "O shrieve me, shrieve me, holy man!"

MASKS ANCIENT AND MODERN

Carnival customs are also reminiscent of ancient pagan ritual practices—particularly initiation rites—in which things are turned upside down. People with higher status take the stance of someone in a lower station and vice versa; men become women, women become men; young people are old and old people are young. A shy person becomes the life of the party; a submissive person orders others about. Like the prince and the pauper of Mark Twain's story of young men living each other's lives, the masked role gives a person a perspective that can be liberating and enlightening. At its best, this experience can increase one's capacity for seeing through the eyes of another and render the person more compassionate in all human relations.

When the boundaries are clearly understood, interaction among strangers who wear various masks in cyberspace serves in much the same way that the mask of Carnival or the theatre does, giving an opportunity to express aspects of identity that are subordinate or unconscious. Hiding behind a mask makes it possible to release real feelings or behaviors into an arena of fantasy. When a paraplegic man logs on as a Navy Seal, for example, he is able, through this misrepresentation of the facts, to speak out of parts of himself that have no other means of expression.

Sometimes, however, this slanted portrayal is just plain lying. In this form of deception and self-deception, participants transgress or ignore the normal protocol for getting acquainted and developing a relationship. Often, such encounters involve a sexual element. Such was the case for Kyla, who described to me how she entered a virtual relationship in a chat room. Gradually the boundaries that contained and defined this relationship were eroded, and her deceptive behavior seeped into real life, jeopardizing her real-life relationships.

Kyla was in her early thirties when she signed into her first chat room on the Internet. Her ten-year marriage was caving under the pressures created by financial stress; the needs of her three children; and her husband's long, late hours at work. Feeling frustrated, unappreciated, and lonely night after night, she went to her computer for adult human companionship. She was fascinated to discover that she could construct a personal profile according to the type of man whom she wanted to attract. She writes:

> I could create myself as a goddess, or just the average female. It didn't matter what I looked like, what part of the country I was from, or what my annual income was. It all had to do with the possibility of chat. Chat would start very casually. Each of us would introduce ourselves. I found myself telling lies about my age, appearance, and marital status, as I sought to be attractive to the men in the chat. Then, as we continued to write, we shared more about our personal lives, frustrations, dreams, and goals. With one man, Sean, the chat eventually got into a discussion of

sexual desires. We talked about our likes and dislikes in the bedroom. I became sexually excited as he asked me questions about what my fantasies were. Did I have desires that had never been fulfilled? Then it became a personal exchange. When I expressed my erotic desires, we went to the next stage, where we sought to satisfy each other's desires in a process called "cybersex." We would send messages back and forth, expressing in detail what we could do to one another. At some point, masturbation would escalate the chat that was between the two of us. I wanted to have Sean close to me—so much so that my imagination could bring me to climax. I felt as though this person was the only person in my life. I was desired, loved, and beautiful, and I felt less lonely. My desire to talk with Sean became an obsession, and we scheduled conversations by telephone. To me, a relationship had formed. We had shared something together that meant that I was important to him. Although we had not even seen one another's bodies, we were having a cyber-affair.

But what I didn't really take into consideration is that this man who had become my closest companion was a stranger. I didn't know whether he was telling me the truth about his life, any more than I had told the truth about mine. The intimacy was so important to me at the time, it didn't make any difference to me. All I knew was that I needed to talk to Sean again and again. I needed to see those words on the screen. The words that made me feel wanted.

Eventually, I realized that my Internet affair had gotten out of hand. Not only was I being dishonest with Sean, but I was avoiding the issues in my marriage. I told him the truth, then I changed my e-mail address and sought counseling for my sake and the sake of my relationships with my husband and children. Now, two years later (and happier in my marriage), I feel ashamed of what I did, but I will not forget how close I felt to Sean (or whatever his name was), a man I never met.

Kyla's cyberaffair began as a foray into fantasy. Like so many others who explore relationships on the Internet, she logged on to an AOL chat room thinking that it would be like a game. She had even considered taking on the personae of a man, but she chose instead to be herself (albeit twenty-five pounds lighter, a few years younger, unmarried, and unencumbered by three young children). When Kyla recognized that she had crossed a boundary between fantasy and reality, she severed the relationship that had gone awry and turned her attention to her real-life relationships.

THE KINDNESS OF STRANGERS

Weaving through all these accounts of intimacy among anonymous strangers is a theme of spontaneous expression of compassion and acceptance. In such a context, the threat of rejection is minimized because there is less at stake for both parties. The experience of being accepted by another creates a sense of grace at work, embracing us and inviting us into self-acceptance.

Theologian Paul Tillich speaks of having "the courage to accept oneself as accepted in spite of being unacceptable." He goes on to say, "Self-affirmation in spite of the anxiety of guilt and condemnation presupposes participation in something which transcends the self."[3] Indeed, our experience of acceptance does not mean that we are without guilt and imperfection; it just means that we can live in the open, where the optimum conditions for personal and spiritual growth prevail. Curiously, it is our own acceptance of our unacceptable self that opens the way for change or self-improvement, because it highlights the issues we need to confront and gives us a loving context for dealing with them.

When an anonymous encounter, in person or in another setting, makes it possible for us to grow in this kind of self-acceptance, it works on behalf of individual spiritual growth and human community. On the other hand, anonymity poisoned with deception is a dangerous invitation to the violation of other human beings. Even if the participants do not intend to be manipulative, their ruse functions to divide them from their own integrity, and their behavior undermines the foundation of trust that maintains and strengthens human community.

There are some specific guidelines, then, that might be formulated as we distinguish which of our anonymous or near-anonymous encounters with strangers are life-giving and which are destructive or self-indulgent. Whether we enter a professional relationship; attend an anonymous support meeting; or meet by chance on a plane, on the

Internet, or in a park, we have the potential to give and receive the kind of acceptance that is touched by grace, so long as we are able to be honest with ourselves and those we encounter. This does not mean that we disclose every secret of our lives; it means that we do not intentionally deceive or mislead someone. On occasion, we may put on a mask and "conceal ourselves in order to reveal ourselves," but this masking is not done dishonestly and is not confused with real life. Rather, it occurs within mutually understood boundaries, and we recognize that it functions to acquaint us with aspects of our own personality.

We are, it seems, a community of strangers, commissioned by a power that transcends us to be present for one another on behalf of healing, cleansing, and freeing our imperfect selves. Call that power God; call it Spirit; call it Love. Call it what you will, but recognize and employ its power to bring broken individuals together for the sake of a more caring world community.

Why is it that we sometimes divulge our secret longing, our deepest wound, or our nagging tug of shame to someone we have never met and know nothing about?

CHAPTER SEVEN

SHADOWS AND STRANGERS

HOLDING MY LITTLE BLUE SHOPPING BASKET OF SHAM-poo, conditioner, and Epsom salts, I approached the checkout counter at the drugstore, where there was one person ahead of me. I had a meeting nearby at 2:30 P.M. My watch registered 2:10—plenty of time to make the meeting. My attention turned to the woman in front of me in line. Her voice was getting louder as she said to the clerk: "That's not right! It's on sale for $4.66."

"No," answered the young woman punching numbers on the cash register, "it's $10.99." The irate customer insisted the sign on the shelf said the item was on sale, so the sales clerk stepped over to the shelf and checked it. It was $10.99. The item next to it was on sale. The customer scolded her for having the sign in the wrong place (which it wasn't), and said, "Well, I'm certainly not going to pay that much for it." Since she had already rung up the bill, the clerk had to write up a credit. She had some problems with that but finally got it right. She asked the customer to sign it and write down her phone number.

"I'm not giving out my phone number," she insisted, the volume in her voice going up another notch or two. "I don't give anyone my phone number. I have an unlisted number because I get too many calls." She looked at me and repeated, "I just get too many calls."

After the first few minutes of this conversation, I was getting very restless. I would be late to my meeting. The line was getting longer. The containers of Epsom salts were getting heavier. Behind me, a customer let out a deep sigh, noisily threw her items on the counter, and stomped out the door. I considered leaving, too.

As I became more and more agitated, I took my own spiritual temperature. At that point, I just observed. I observed myself mostly; also the clerk and the difficult customer. I awakened to myself in that moment and to the negative feelings that were on the rise. This brief inner glance did wonders. I stopped tapping my fingers and looking at my watch. I admired the clerk, who was warm in her manner as she spoke to the customer.

When the sale was finally completed and the woman had left, I just smiled at the clerk and gave her my items. "Thank you for your patience," she said. I looked at her directly and said, "Modeled by yours."

As I hurried to my meeting, now ten minutes late, I got behind a driver who was going about twenty-five miles per hour in a thirty-five zone. "You idiot," I exclaimed, now too frustrated and hurried to bother taking my internal temperature, "Speed up or get off the road!"

DR. JEKYLL AND MR. HYDE TIED UP IN TRAFFIC

It would not have occurred to me to be rude to the sales clerk in the drugstore, but things were different when I got behind the wheel of my car. I am reminded of one of those didactic films you have to watch when you apply for a reduction in your insurance rates or a decrease in your penalty on a driving violation—the one where a Casper Milquetoast Mr. Niceguy has a personality change when he gets in his car. Apparently Dr. Jekyll and Mr. Hyde are alive and well, re-created daily in traffic tussles all over the world. Road rage, a term that entered our vocabulary some time during the last decade of the twentieth century, is on the rise. In fact, it is the number one traffic problem in the United States. In a typical road rage scenario, Driver A tailgates Driver B for a half-mile before an additional lane presents the opportunity to pass. Driver B, irritated with the tailgater, speeds up so Driver A cannot pass. Driver A then speeds up enough to get in front of Driver B and hits the brakes. Driver B slams on the brakes, barely avoiding a collision.

Although we may not all go so far as to act out our hostility in an overt interaction of road rage, I suspect that most of us have had the opportunity to get acquainted with some of the less attractive aspects of ourselves when we drive a vehicle. For me, it was the city of Boston that held up the mirror and introduced me to Mr. Hyde.

When I moved to Boston to begin my studies at Harvard Divinity School, I soon discovered that going to school in Boston included getting informal training in traffic combat. Apparently there were some rules of the road peculiar to the Boston area.

The first rule of Boston driving appeared to be, "Don't make eye contact." This rule was especially accommodating to those who cut into the flow of traffic without regard for other vehicles already occupying their lane of choice.

Another rule was, "Don't ever, ever stop at a yellow light." That's because you will surely be rear-ended by the six cars behind you who plan to "make" the light.

The rule that was the hardest for me to accept, however, was the one that applied to making turns. Road wisdom dictated that if you are driving in the left lane, be ever conscious of drivers in the right lane who want to make a left turn. You must be ready at any moment to hit your brakes as they turn in front of you.

After several close calls, eliciting gestures and expletives I did not know I was even capable of using, I found myself fantasizing that I might purchase a big old 1969 Cadillac and drive it through Boston like a tank. Instead of searing my brake linings yielding to the person in the shiny BMW who didn't make eye contact, I would stare straight ahead, maintain speed, and aim for no more than a dent in my fender. It would be sort of like playing bumper cars at Disneyland.

Mind you, I was studying for the ministry. These were not nice thoughts for someone who was about to don her clerical garb and stained-glass smile.

The rule of *don't look* is perhaps the most common element in traffic confrontation everywhere. If you do not make eye contact with other drivers, you are better able to distance yourself from their humanity. For that matter, you can lose touch with your own humanity.

The strategy of avoiding eye contact also seems to apply to heavily populated city sidewalks. When I lived in London, for example, walking was my primary mode of transportation, and I frequently negotiated the High Street at rush hours. Since there were no proper lanes or speed limits for pedestrians, it was sometimes a challenge to avoid a collision. Even young mothers pushing their baby strollers learned how to play chicken, invariably forcing those in their path to yield. Not only did most people plow ahead without regard for my space, but most of them appeared to have mobile (cell) phones permanently affixed to their ear. In spite of the competition for space on the sidewalk, however, most people did not lose their cool. They just said "Sorry" when they bumped into me and went on their way.

Another dynamic occurred with automobiles. In England, pedestrians can step into a zebra crossing, marked by black and white poles supporting yellow globe-lamps that flash continuously; law dictates that any car approaching the crossing must stop. It was rare for any driver to ignore this particular law. But on one occasion, I came close to being hit by a driver who failed to stop. He was well out of hearing distance as I thanked him unkindly for making my day a little more exciting than usual.

There are not many of us, I suspect, who have not at least mouthed a few angry words in the direction of a stranger. Sometimes the degree to which we vent our anger is less in response to their offense and more a reflection of our own state of mind. For example, about a month after the terrorist attacks of September 11, 2001, Marilyn Sewell, a minister of a large congregation in Portland, Oregon, was feeling deeply affected by the horror of those events. Although she usually cried easily, she had not yet been able to cry. Showing classic symptoms of grief and response to trauma, she could not concentrate well, and her sleep was interrupted by unsettling dreams. She also felt anger that would simply rise up, sometimes when she was least aware of it.

One such occasion occurred as she was walking in her neighborhood. A driver was about to go through a stop sign while she was crossing the street. Shaking her fist at him, she shouted, "Asshole!" About ten feet farther along, a woman who was standing in her yard greeted Marilyn. "Hello, Dr. Sewell," she said.

I can only imagine how mortified Marilyn was to have someone recognize her and witness her angry lapse. The fact is, Marilyn was not that angry with the driver who appeared to be running the stop sign. She was burdened with a more complex anger, mixed with grief, confusion, and frustration. The tears she could not force found their way into her clenched fist. The errant driver became the enemy she could not confront.

Our hostility or aggression toward strangers in the street is usually less about them and more about us. With the insulation we create through anonymity, however, they are the convenient target of our anger and frustration. If, as Marilyn did, we suffer with anger that erupts in a way we neither understand nor know how to express, we are more likely to project it onto the stranger. In most cases, particularly if our curses and gestures are not really intended for their eyes and ears, we do not have to be accountable—at least not to them. We are, of course, accountable to our selves, and to the Spirit that calls us into alignment with our values of compassion and kindness.

This came home to Curt, a friend of mine who was cut off by another driver as he entered the Lincoln Tunnel. As was his habit, he directed a few vocal expletives toward the offender. The words were out before he noticed that both of them were driving with the window open; the other driver heard the unpleasant appellations. Curt felt his face turning red with embarrassment as the driver made eye contact and smiled smugly. Although he did not have to interact further with the other man, he cringed to have a layer of his anonymity peeled away, exposing the angry voice within.

FLAMING INTO TELESPACE

Telephone solicitors are also an easy mark for a rude outburst. They interrupt us at inconvenient times and are usually promoting something we do not want. I recently conducted an informal survey among some of the phone solicitors who called me. "What kind of response do you usually get from people?" I asked. They reported that people usually just hang up. Some yell at the caller, demanding that they be put on a do-not-call list. Others listen a bit, offer a few words of abrupt dismissal ("Sorry, not interested"), and then hang up. One of the people I interviewed said, "Well, that's just the way people are; I don't let it bother me."

Sometimes, however, telephone solicitors reach their limits. When we lived in New York, my husband Chuck responded to a call very politely, explaining that he really was not interested in whatever it was the man was promoting. Chuck was surprised when the caller yelled at him, "All you New Yorkers are assholes!" Dumbfounded and incredulous, Chuck just stood there for a minute holding the receiver, as the dial tone buzzed in his ear.

Several years ago, I went to a workshop led by Buddhist monk and teacher Thich Nhat Hanh. I don't remember much that he said, but I remember his presence. He embodied mindfulness and compassion and peace and warmth. He said we have to smile to ourselves because we need our own compassion. One thing I remember is his suggestion that we practice mindfulness with a telephone meditation. When the phone rings, don't answer it until the third or fourth ring. Stay where you are and breathe in and out. As you breathe in, say "I calm myself," and as you breathe out, say "I smile." On the third ring, move toward the phone. By the time you pick up the receiver, you are in a more pleasant and peaceful state of mind.

I tried the telephone meditation for about a week, I think, before I went back to the same old mindless habits. Since then, however, I have been more mindful about how I speak with strangers on the phone, especially telephone solicitors. Such calls test my patience, to be sure, and mindful conversation gives me some perspective on how I regard both my time and theirs. Instead of hanging up, which would save me maybe a minute or two of my precious time, I listen briefly; then I offer a polite dismissal. If the person does not accept my declaration that I do not wish to hear more, I tell her or him again, maintaining composure and trying to think about what that person's perspective and experience might be. I have come to think of this exercise as sort of a ministry of manners.

Regardless of the effect this response has on the caller, it is good for my spirit (and my body, since anger and stress have a way of taking a toll there, too). Like Thich Nhat Hanh's telephone meditation, it centers me in the source of peace that makes me present to all interactions, even those I do not welcome. Disciplining myself to listen for a minute creates consciousness of my own impatience and gives me an occasion to get perspective on myself. Yes, I value my time, but I also cherish the space where I interact with another person, no matter who that person is. It is the soul's classroom. In that space, I am humbled, for I must learn over and over again to respect the personhood of even the most obnoxious individual at the other end of a telephone connection.

Another ready venue for displaced anger is our online connections. My e-mail program has a function called "Moodwatch." With the appearance of the icon that shows a couple of red chili peppers, it asks, "About to send a red-hot e-mail? Check yourself with Moodwatch." I admit it: I have hit the *send* button on more than one message that would have rated about two-and-a-half chili peppers on a scale of one to three, and I regretted it. People write what they do not say, and the convenience of e-mail has resulted in many of us using our computers for conversations that might better be conducted in person or on the telephone (or not at all). In effect, we separate ourselves from a more personal interaction and make ourselves vulnerable to the temptation to write what we might not be willing to say face-to-face. Technology becomes our insulation from an honest and responsible confrontation.

I recall speaking with a friend who is the chief operating officer for a large company in New York City. When the Love Bug virus infected the company's computer system, the staff had to pick up the phone or walk across the hall instead of using e-mail. This refreshing interlude of personal interaction generated energy and warmth in the office; it inspired him to think about how to encourage face-to-face interaction among his staff after the virus was expelled.

Avoidance or cowardice is further encouraged in other settings in cyberspace. In Chapter Six, I discussed use of the Internet for exploring intimate relationships. Likewise, the anonymity available through online connection has led to expressions of anger called "flaming," the name used for rude invective and tirades hurled across cyberspace. Flame throwers take their version of road rage to the information highway, where they project their anger on strangers and do not have to face each other in a direct confrontation. A typical incident might start with someone in a newsgroup chat making a statement that is insensitive toward, say, the Latino community. Someone then writes a few scathing words back to this "racist pig," and then a few others join in the flame war, pouncing on either the blunderer or the flame thrower. In his book *Bowling Alone,* Robert Putnam points out the effect of this kind of interaction: "Anonymity and fluidity in the virtual world encourage 'easy in, easy out,' 'drive-by' relationships. That very casualness is the appeal of computer-mediated communication for some denizens of cyberspace. . . . If entry and exit are too easy, commitment, trustworthiness, and reciprocity will not develop."[1]

Indeed, the nature of interaction on the Internet not only discourages relationships of trust and commitment; it also fails to hold people accountable to a common code of conduct. Hence, it is easy to allow displaced anger to ride on the cybercurrents of anonymity, where it further erodes the bonds of civility that strengthen our social network and our human community.

THE POISON TREE OF DISPLACED ANGER

The anger that erupts in road rage and other aggressive interactions with strangers can leak into our more intimate associations if we fail to find a constructive way to express it. There it spreads like venom in the body and soul. William Blake's poem, "A Poison Tree," describes how this lethal toxin infects our relationships:

I was angry with my friend:
I told my wrath, my wrath did end.
I was angry with my foe:
I told it not, my wrath did grow.

And I water'd it in fears
Night & morning with my tears;
And I sunned it with smiles,
And with soft deceitful wiles.

And it grew both day and night,
Till it bore an apple bright;
And my foe beheld it shine,
And he knew that it was mine,

And into my garden stole
When the night had veil'd the pole:
In the morning glad I see
My foe outstretch'd beneath the tree.[2]

As Blake's poem illustrates, anger expressed in the context of a caring relationship nurtures true intimacy. It only becomes dangerous when it is harbored and fed with our fears, our tears, and our deceitful wiles.

Intimacy comes from a Latin word that means "innermost." To achieve intimacy, we need to be authentic and vulnerable. Anger is, of course, part of any intimate relationship. If it is not expressed in some way, the intimacy diminishes. Without space for anger, the appearance of a nice, smooth relationship is likely to be a cover for a stagnant coexistence. Many people who successfully suppress their anger eventually turn it inward, where it not only stifles relationships but contributes to depression, high blood pressure, an ulcer, or other health problems.

Then there are those at the other extreme. These are people who are always expressing their anger. Some have been abused or abandoned, and their prickly barbs protect them from being hurt more. Just like those who retreat into silence, they likewise insulate themselves from intimacy—with their anger. Sometimes they take up a social cause because it offers them a legitimate channel for their anger; they can be angry for someone else instead of themselves, thus distancing themselves from the source of the anger. They do good work, but the fact remains that their deeper anger has not been recognized. Slow to forgive, they may hold onto a grudge for years and years, avoiding intimacy in a relationship.

At both extremes—those who suppress anger and those who wear it like a porcupine coat—there is one thing in common: the angry person does not part with the anger, and it becomes a protective shield against intimate relationship.

Managing anger, says Carol Tavris, "depends on taking responsibility for one's emotions and one's actions: on refusing the temptation, for instance, to remain stuck in blame and fury or silent resentment. Once anger becomes a force to berate the nearest scapegoat instead of to change a bad situation, it loses its credibility and its power. It feeds only on itself. And it sure as sunrise makes for a grumpy life."[3]

Displaced anger insulates us from intimacy, and it erupts in our encounters with strangers as well. It is clearly the sort that "becomes a force to berate the nearest scapegoat." Unable to express it appropriately among our closest companions, we unleash it on those who are in less of a position to hurt us.

It is important to understand our own anger because the anger we keep or feed finds expression in the most destructive and violent ways, just as the anger we examine and release in a caring context enables us to correct an injustice, change ourselves, and heal a broken relationship.

As we examine our own anger, we see that in some cases we can do something to change our situation. In other cases, we cannot. We cannot change other people, we cannot change the past, and we cannot express our anger to someone who is no longer alive. In many cases, we know it is not productive to express it to someone who *is* alive. So sometimes we just have to let go of it. Talking about it is one way to do that. Prayer or ritual may be helpful. Sometimes we can even forgive someone who has never asked for our forgiveness—because we need to do it. (Forgiveness, it is said, is giving up all hope for a better past.) I am not saying we do any of this easily. But I am saying that if we do not find a way to let go, we eat away at ourselves and our anger becomes indirectly destructive in relationships. The task is to identify anger, understand it, and use it to correct the injustices that provoke it. The task is to use it rather than be used by it.

"Who knows what evil lurks in the hearts of men? The Shadow knows!"

In the days before television, Lamont Cranston made these words familiar, as he presented the radio classic "The Shadow." Nowadays we try to be inclusive with our language, so we admit that there might be some evil lurking in the hearts of women, too. Lamont Cranston's Shadow, however (our image for the dark side of human nature), is the invisible force for good. This would suggest that the shadow (that is, the Mr. Hyde in us all) has the potential to be a force for good. I think it does.

Psychoanalyst Carl Jung talked about the shadow as something that does not have to come out in destructive behavior. It is just something inside that we would prefer not be there—something that doesn't fit into our picture of our ideal self. Usually it is not-so-acceptable feelings like anger or jealousy or bigotry. The shadow is not really so dangerous if we recognize it and stay acquainted with it. It becomes dangerous when we lose touch with it (which is very easy to do) and consequently distance ourselves from the ability to see the humanity in others. No one is immune. An experience I had many years ago is a reminder of how easily the shadow creeps into our behavior without our awareness of how it operates.

My husband and I were in our late twenties when we joined a church. We were newcomers and didn't know anyone well, so we signed up for the annual retreat held by the church's young couples group.[4]

We played volleyball and cooked out and did the things people do when they go on retreat. Then we settled in by a fire for an evening of fun and games.

A visitor to the group introduced a game called "Choo Choo." It starts with one person passing through a room full of people, going "Choo, choo, choo, choo," like a train, and choosing a member of the opposite sex and choo-chooing into another room. Then the two of them come choo-chooing in and the second person selects someone and they choo-choo on into the other room. And so on. Because I didn't get picked until almost the end, I got to watch as several people choo-chooed through. I also grew curious as the choo-choo train took longer and longer in the other room. It would be quiet for a while, then I could hear laughter.

Finally my turn came, and choo-choo I went at the end of the long line. When we got into the other room, we stopped and the first person kissed the second one, who kissed the next one, and so on. When it came to my turn, the man in front of me took his position for the kiss, then slapped me on the cheek. Then everyone laughed, and we choo-chooed on in to pick up the next unsuspecting person. When it came my turn to slap him, I offered only a light pat on the cheek. But I did participate. I was relieved when the game was over, and I went to bed early, somewhat disenchanted with the fun and games of the evening.

I found out later that this choo-choo experience was devastating for the woman who was the last person to be picked. Somehow I had forgotten—blocked out in my mind—how the game ended. When her turn came, she did not want to participate, but she went along reluctantly into the next room. Stunned by the slap, she was unprepared for what would happen next. The visitor who had introduced the game pinned her to the wall: "Up against the wall, bitch!" he said, preparing to reward her with a kiss she did not want. I don't remember if I joined others in laughter. I hope I didn't.

There we were at a church retreat, passengers on a choo-choo train that was out of control and headed for disaster. Later, when some of us spoke of the experience with shame and regret, we were still inclined to blame the visitor for getting us involved in this cruel game. It was hard to look at ourselves and take responsibility for an evening that went awry.

This subtle and insidious dynamic of group behavior reminds me of William Golding's classic novel *Lord of the Flies,* the disturbing tale of what happens to a group of boys from a proper British school who are stranded on an island. These very civilized youngsters begin their island life with orderly and democratic meetings and the appropriate pause for afternoon tea. They elect Ralph their chief, but a rivalry develops between Ralph and the leader of the choir, Jack. Some of the children see something they think is a beast, and they became more and more frightened of the threats of the jungle. As fear mounts, more of the boys join up with Jack, whose choir has become a "tribe" of hunters, and they stalk and kill a wild pig. They chant, "Kill the beast, cut his throat, spill his blood!" Then, in a frenzy of celebrating the slaughter, they go out of control and kill one of their own members, Simon. Later, another boy, Piggy, is murdered when one of the members of the hunting tribe sends a large boulder crashing upon him. By the time the boys are finally rescued, Jack and his tribe have set fire to the island and, with spears poised in pursuit, are hunting Ralph, the last civilized soul.

The book's title, *Lord of the Flies,* is an English translation of the Hebrew "Ba'alzevuv," which means "chief of the insects" or, in its Greek form, Beelzebub, chief of the devils. In the book, the lord of the flies refers to the head of the pig that the boys slaughter; the head is impaled on a stick. Before he is murdered, the innocent boy Simon encounters it. In an imaginary conversation, the pig's head speaks to Simon, saying, "Fancy thinking the Beast was something you could hunt and kill! . . . You knew, didn't you? I'm part of you? Close, close, close!"[5]

It's a powerful story. Golding's point is clear. The beast is inside the most innocent of the boys, Simon. The beast was inside of my companions and me as we played Choo Choo at a church retreat. The beast. Beelzebub. The power of evil itself. Close, close, close.

When we do not recognize how close, the shadow becomes most dangerous, for that is when we cast it onto others, usually strangers, demonizing them, perhaps hating them, and then seeking to destroy them.

LOVE YOUR ENEMY

A friend asked me, "Where do they find them all? . . . I'm talking about the executioners, the torturers, and the dehumanizers that do the bidding of the power wielders—Osama bin Laden, Saddam Hussein,

Hitler, Pol Pot, Khomeini, Idi Amin, Stalin. Is the human being basically 'bad' until put under internal and social control? Are both behavior and feelings learned?"

The man who posed these questions lost some of his own family members to the Nazi horror of the 1930s and 1940s. His question touches the core of our faith, where we consider the human potential for evil and good, and affirm the power of redemption in every human soul.

I do not know where "they" find those people who steer airplanes into buildings and murder thousands of people; those people who send explosive materials or deadly diseases through the mail; those people who torture, those people who sell drugs to children, those people who do the bidding of the Hitlers of our world. I suspect that many of those people were not so fortunate as I was and may not have grown up embraced by the loving attention of wise and virtuous parents. I suspect that many of them learned violence as the victim of violence in their family, or by living where violence is a daily reality. Maybe they believed they were doing good, just as the witch hunters and inquisitors of past centuries who murdered thousands of people in the name of God thought they were doing good. Maybe they believed in the cause of their country, just as many who have slaughtered children in war believed it was for a good and just cause.

What I do believe about those people is that they were capable of torturing another human being because they had lost touch with what made them human. They were capable of causing another person to suffer great pain because they had shut away their own pain.

Another thing I believe about them: they were, or are, the agents—and victims—of something evil.

Abraham Joshua Heschel wrote that there is no human being "who does not carry a treasure in the soul." I believe this affirmation too, and that includes those people—bin Laden, Hitler, Hussein; the terrorists, the skinheads, the bigots, the torturers, the evildoers. There is no human being who does not carry a treasure in the soul. The Quakers call it the divine light within every person. If we cannot see any sign of it, then we are called upon to offer the most sacred kind of love. In so doing, we may not be able to redeem them, but we redeem ourselves from hatred. Love your enemy. Love your enemy not because it redeems your enemy, but because it redeems you.

Observing the cruel behavior of human beings, Mark Twain called us "the damned human race." We are, he said, the only creatures who inflict pain "for the pleasure of doing it."[6] Yes, we humans do terrible things that the "higher" animals do not. Strip away our civilized exterior, and we are like those boys on the island in *Lord of the Flies*.

Or are we? Time after time we hear stories of heroism—of people like the firemen and ordinary citizens who risked or lost their lives in their effort to rescue victims of the 2001 terrorist attack on the World Trade Center. I shall never forget the remarkable courage of a man who plunged into the freezing waters of the Potomac River to rescue victims of an Air Florida plane that crashed into a bridge in 1982. In the aftermath of any war, there are those who are remembered for acts of genuine sacrifice and love. War, which brings out the worst in people, can also bring out the best.

These people who have done exceptional things are not necessarily exceptional people. They are people who found themselves in circumstances where they acted not upon a reasoned course but upon some instinctive—call it primitive—urge to respond on behalf of life.

Memorable words from the diary of Anne Frank, written less than three weeks before her capture by Nazis in 1944, come to mind: "It's difficult in times like these: ideals, dreams and cherished hopes rise within us, only to be crushed by grim reality. It's a wonder I haven't abandoned all my ideals, they seem so absurd and impractical. Yet I cling to them because I still believe, in spite of everything, that people are truly good at heart."[7]

Yes the beast is there—close, close, close! It is essential to know that—to recognize the beast within. The seeds of violence are there in each of us, and we nourish them with our ignorance of their presence and our failure to see the potential for evil. Today it may be road rage or a kissing game; tomorrow it could be rounding up Muslims or Arab Americans and putting them in concentration camps.

The beast is the stranger inside who feeds on fear and stirs hatred in our hearts. It is when we are estranged from this stranger that we are at peril. But the light of the divine Spirit is there too—close, close, close!

Love your enemy.
Love your enemy not because
it redeems your enemy,
but because it redeems you.

CHAPTER EIGHT

HOSPITALITY
THE GIFT OF PRESENCE

AUTHOR DAVID RANKIN TELLS THE STORY OF A TIME when he stopped at a restaurant for a quick meal. It was one of those places that catered to what he calls "confused tourists and local residents who had pawned their taste buds." I have been in many similar greasy spoon eateries, and I can imagine the scene that Rankin observed when a server took orders for a table where the customers appeared to be a mother, a father, and a young son. She wrote the orders for the parents and then turned to the child:

"What will you have?" she asked the boy.

"I want a hot dog! . . ." the boy began.

"No hot dog!" the mother interrupted. "Give him what we ordered!"

The waitress ignored her.

"Do you want anything on your hot dog?" she asked.

"Ketchup!" the boy replied with a happy smile.

"Coming up!" she said, as she walked to the kitchen.

There was silence at the table.

Then the youngster said to his mother: "Mom, she thinks I'm real!"[1]

Sometimes it is a stranger, even more than someone close to us, who is able to recognize and affirm who we are—to acknowledge that yes, we are "real." Buddhist teacher Thich Nhat Hanh says that the most precious gift we can give to anyone is our presence. In the Christian tradition, this gift of presence is at the core of the central concept of hospitality. Hospitality is less about what we may do for others than about who we are when we are with them. It is about serving our faith on behalf of the human community in our everyday interactions. Nurturing trust and goodwill, we create a space that holds another person with the deepest kind of respect.

Hospitality is a religious calling for those who choose to live in a monastic community. As a guest in Christian and Buddhist monasteries and the Hindu-based Vedanta community, I have experienced the kind of hospitality that not only honors the bond we share as human beings but also renders presence unobtrusively and graciously. In these monastic or community-oriented settings, I was given space for solitude. The structure of the rituals of each day gave me the freedom to let go of my own routine, opening inner space for renewal and guidance. Meals shared in silence were a communion of emptiness—a bond between people whose quiet absence was their presence, and whose presence was their way of honoring the Spirit.

Offering our presence does not mean that we hold a perpetual open house, either in our physical space or in our hearts. In the Benedictine monastic community, for example, the spiritual practice of hospitality is not an invitation to visitors to have full run of the place. You enter their space with regard for their rules of conduct and their private routines. There is a tension that exists whereby the brothers, adhering to the Rule of St. Benedict, welcome all guests as Christ; at the same time, they maintain the integrity of their community. Although they are isolated from the world and its values, they are not insulated from it. Taking the time to attend to their devotional life individually and as a community helps them be at home enough in themselves to welcome outsiders into their midst.

Although we have come to think of the word *hospitality* in terms of social interaction, its meaning derives from Latin roots shared with several other words. It is interesting to note, for example, that the words *host* and *guest* derive from the same Latin word *hostis*, which refers, in its noun form, to "host, guest, stranger, foreigner." In its original use, it meant "stranger," and in classical use "enemy." (Hence we observe the use of the root form in the word *hostile*.) A variation of the same word is used to refer to the sacrifice of Jesus that is represented in the communion "host." The words *hospital, hospice, hotel,* and *hostel* also derive from the same Latin form.

When I lived in England, I observed that people do not use an article with the word *hospital*. Instead of saying someone is in *the* hospital, they say he or she is "in hospital." The implication is that this is not just a place; it is rather a state of being, a way of being held through suffering. So, too, we might interpret the word *hospitality* as a state of mutual trust into which guest and host enter together. As the root word implies, hospitality to a "guest," in addition to having a mutuality of presence, is also an invitation to the "stranger" or "enemy" to enter one's private realm.

WELCOMING THE STRANGER

"Hospitality," writes Parker Palmer, "links the private and the public life, giving us a way to walk between the two realms. The stranger is found in public, but the means of hospitality are private. Hospitality means inviting the stranger into our private space, whether that be the space of our home or the space of our personal awareness and concern. . . . Hospitality to the stranger gives us a chance to see our own lives afresh, through different eyes."[2]

It is sometimes easier to practice hospitality in the space of personal awareness than in the privacy of home. It is all very well to welcome a stranger into your monastery, where you have guidelines for visitors, but most of us are a little nervous about opening our private homes to someone we do not know. If someone knocks, we may not even be comfortable answering the door, particularly if we are alone. In the city, we have security personnel or protective devices to ensure that we are not bothered by unwanted intruders. In the suburbs, gated communities ensure that all guests are invited guests. Our home is our sanctuary, our safe haven, and we are careful about who enters it.

I admit to being very cautious as I opened my door on a Saturday afternoon several years ago to a strange visitor. As I beheld the frail elderly woman on the stoop, I dismissed any fears for my own safety. I was in the midst of writing my Sunday sermon, however, and was annoyed with any interruption. I stood in the doorway as she attempted to introduce herself. I say attempted, because it became apparent that she had difficulty speaking. Her voice was strained and her pronunciation somewhat garbled. It took a great deal of patience and several requests for repetition before I even understood her name. I wondered if she had become disoriented or was lost—or if perhaps she had walked too far and had run out of steam. I lived on a hill and could not imagine that she had the strength to walk up the steep incline. *Why,* I wondered, *was this woman at my door?*

I invited her to come in and sit down and offered her something to drink. By repeating back to her what I thought she was trying to say and asking questions, I finally found out that she was a neighbor. She knew her way home. There was no emergency. She just wanted someone to talk to. Since I was a rather public person in the community, she knew who I was, so she just decided to come for a visit.

I offered to walk or drive her home, and she said she wanted to walk. Her pace was quite slow, particularly for someone like me, often accused of being on my way to a fire when I get into my stride. She managed the incline just fine, though, and we had more time to talk. When we got to her house, she invited me in and introduced me to her husband, who had Alzheimer's. By this time I was getting better at understanding her speech. Then she showed me photographs of her beloved granddaughter, who had been murdered several years before. She rummaged around in some drawers until she found an article she wanted me to read. It was a piece she had written for the local paper, about how it felt to grow old, how it felt to lose her ability to speak, and about how it felt to be an intelligent articulate person who was repeatedly mistaken for a confused old woman because she could no longer shape her thoughts into clear language.

By the time I walked home, I realized that the hospitality I extended to this neighbor was less about welcoming her into my home than it was about giving her the opportunity to invite me into her home, her life, and her heart. I felt enriched by this encounter with a bright and vital woman of exceptional spirit. I also felt ashamed to think of the stereotypes that I had conjured up on first meeting her.

In practicing genuine hospitality, it often turns out that we are enriched by an exchange with a stranger. In this situation with my neighbor, I also confronted my fear of the strange person at my door and struggled with my impatience. The holy intimacy of this encounter was as much in my confrontation with my own resistance as in the exchange with a frail-looking old woman who could not speak clearly. My sermon may have suffered from the interruption, but my spirit was nourished by her hospitality to me.

NO ROOM AT THE INN

The experience of hospitality that stands out in my memory above all others is one where I was clearly on the receiving end of a gracious gift of presence. I will never forget it.

To begin with, it was an evening in late January 1967, when the Chicago area was visited by the worst snowstorm of the century. I was traveling with three companions—Sally, Mal, and George—with whom I had attended a professional conference. We all worked for Young Life, a Christian ministry to high school youth. We had left Chicago in George's van and made it as far as Valparaiso, Indiana, before the snow became deep enough to close the roads. We tried to find lodging in several hotels, including a sleazy fleabag in the heart of town where it looked as though they would rent rooms by the hour. There was not a single bed to be had. The roads were lined with truckers camped in their cabs for the night. We tried calling a few churches, but there was no answer. Since there was a university in town, we decided to head for the dormitories and see if the students might have a warm corner for us. Meanwhile the blizzard winds sculpted the snow into six-foot drifts.

Driving through the campus we saw some students walking on the road and stopped to ask directions. We told them we were hoping to find a place to stay in a dormitory.

"Come to my house," one of them said without hesitation. "We have plenty of room." He said good-bye to his companions and hopped in the van with us. In a few moments we were inside the large drafty Victorian house that he shared with three other men, two of whom were there when we arrived. The third, Sandy, was at a party and would not be in until quite late.

Before we retired for the evening, we sat around a fire in the parlor and talked with Jay, Nick, and Stefan. I don't recall much from the conversation, except that we told the students about our work and what it meant to us, which led to deeper probing into questions of faith, doubt, and inner longing. Our hosts seemed hungry to explore topics like the existence of God, the teachings of Jesus, and the struggle to live according to ethical values.

Sally and I were assigned to Sandy's room for the night. Sandy was informed about his generosity when he came home from his party and saw a note posted on his door. He tiptoed around us as he came in to gather some personal items; I felt like Goldilocks intruding on Baby Bear.

In the morning, we awoke to the smell of sausage and pancakes, with Jay, our first host, showing off his flipping expertise. Sandy got up too late for breakfast, but he smiled with pleasure when we thanked him for his involuntary hospitality. "No problem," he said. "I can't wait to tell my friends that there were two strange women in my bed when I got home."

The roads were open by late morning, and we prepared to leave. Like a mother hen, Jay handed us a large bag packed with sandwiches, fruit, and cookies—provisions for the journey.

We gushed with gratitude to these students who had rescued us from winter's fury and had given us more than a warm place to sleep. They gushed right back, as they told us what a gift our visit was to them, too.

It doesn't always work out that way, but when it does, I believe the Spirit gives us a glimpse of what is possible among us. We learn as much from our need for help from strangers as we do from the times we are inspired to reach out to help them.

THE GIFT OF TRUST

In a situation similar to my encounter in Valparaiso, Gary Smith, a United Church of Christ (UCC) minister at the time, found himself in need of help from a stranger. He and his wife and their one-year-old son were traveling through the Shenandoah Valley on their way home to Connecticut. They stopped for dinner and were on their way to their motel when his wife said she was not feeling well. She was not feeling well at all.

Her condition worsened, and by early morning Gary had piled her and their son into the car, heading for the hospital emergency room. As they sped through the small town, Gary spotted a UCC church. He noted the name of the church and its minister.

While hospital personnel treated his wife, Gary went to the phone in the waiting room. It was 6:30 in the morning as he dialed the number of the local UCC minister.

Gary went right to the point as he introduced himself. "I'm Gary Smith, and I'm a UCC minister. We stopped for the night in your town, and my wife is in the midst of a medical emergency. I have a one-year-old son, and I need you to come and take him to your home for the day."

Within minutes, a man Gary had never met arrived at the hospital, they exchanged greetings and essential information, and then Gary watched as the minister walked out the door with his baby boy. Gary later reflected on this encounter: "My wife was hospitalized for three days. That minister and his family went to the motel and gathered up our belongings and brought them to their home, where my son and I stayed until we could all resume our journey. Aside from a gift and a letter of thanks we sent right away, I have never seen them again and do not remember their names. It does not matter."

What mattered was that Gary trusted his baby to someone he did not know, relying on a bond they shared as colleagues and men of compassion. What mattered was that their exchange brought them into sacred space, where trust prevails and the human bond draws from its deepest resources. What mattered was that when Gary needed God's presence at 6:30 A.M. in a strange town, it was only a phone call away.

A STRANGER WHO CARES

Experiences like Gary's and mine are not, I suspect, really unusual. Most people can recall at least one time in their lives when they were in need of help, had to turn to a stranger, and felt embraced in the heart of hospitality as they exchanged gifts of self. We do not go seeking out such encounters; they are thrust upon us by circumstance. It is not, after all, our nature to trust a stranger. When we do, however, we open ourselves to the unexpected gifts of grace. These gifts are not just rendered to us from outside ourselves by generous people; they also work inside us, showing the way to becoming more grateful, generous, and open-hearted in all of our relationships. Humbled by our own need, we let down some of our barriers of self-sufficiency or pride and learn how to receive. Our posture of vulnerability is an invitation to the Spirit to enter our hearts and touch our souls.

The phrase "a stranger who cares" comes to mind as I consider the dynamic that occurs when we are thrust into a relationship by circumstances of misfortune. It was a man named Darrell who used this phrase when he gave me the opportunity to spend time with him through his final weeks of living.

Darrell had a rare and vicious form of cancer. When he was admitted to the hospital where I worked as a chaplain, he had been diagnosed only a few days before. He had been chopping wood and assumed that the sore spot under his arm was a pulled muscle. Suddenly he found himself isolated for a few days with a radiation implant. He was only thirty-nine years old.

I met him shortly before the isolation, and it was clear that he was still in shock. A few days earlier, he was chopping wood. Now, fearing for his life, he felt an agonizing loneliness that went too deep for words.

Radiation had no effect on his fast-growing malignancy, and the next course of treatment was inpatient chemotherapy, using a product that was so lethal, his gums bled continuously. He declined visibly each day. Although it has been twenty years since I made my daily visits with him during that last month of his life, I recall vividly how the crucible of trust into which he poured his pain brought us into holy space together. I sometimes cried myself to sleep as I prayed for the miracle that would heal his emaciated body. What I received in answer to my prayers was not the miracle I requested; it was, rather, the ability to be present with Darrell through the physical and emotional agony he had to endure.

On one occasion, he looked at me with gratitude that was tinged with sadness. "You are a stranger who cares," he said. Then he cried as he told me that his family was not able to be present with him. His teenage son did not come to visit; even his minister made only one perfunctory call. "My wife visits me, but we just talk about treatments or what is happening at home, or what we will do when I get better," he said. "I can't talk about how I really feel. They don't want to hear it."

Late one evening, I received a call from Darrell's doctor. "He won't last much longer," he said. "Please come now." When I arrived at the hospital, Darrell's family, including two brothers who had traveled some distance with their families, were all gathered in the waiting room. I spoke with them first and then started toward Darrell's room. "Oh no," said his wife, "you can't visit him now. If you go in, he will know he is dying."

Apparently Darrell had been told that even the out-of-town relatives who processed through his room for their final visits were all just "passing through" the area. Appalled with this charade, I could have said, "He knows he is dying." Instead, I offered to help them say goodbye and tried to persuade them to let me see him. But his wife was particularly adamant in her insistence that I not go into the room. Seeing her emotional distress, I honored her wishes, very sad indeed that I could not be with him for a final prayer.

THE COURAGE TO BE PRESENT

Darrell's family's failure was not a failure of love; it was apparent to me that they loved him very much. No, it was rather a failure of courage. It takes more than love to be present with someone through suffering and death. To be present is to be willing to be with another person's pain. As a stranger who cared, I was able to do what Darrell's family could not. I could stay with him as he raged, as he uttered his own prayers of desperate loneliness, and as his body and spirit suffered through an assault that I had no power to fix.

I am saddened to think that people who are in the most intimate of family relationships cannot be more present for one another, particularly through times of suffering and death. The failure of courage is, in the long run, a failure to live, which is to say, we fail ourselves as well as those we love when we run away or avoid our own feelings of fear and grief.

In his classic play *Our Town,* Thornton Wilder holds up a mirror to us all in the poignant final scene, where Emily, who has just died in childbirth at the age of twenty-six, is given a chance to relive one day from her life. She chooses her twelfth birthday. After observing only a few minutes of the day, she withdraws. "I can't go on," she says. "It goes so fast. We don't have time to look at one another." After saying goodbye to her town and her family and precious ordinary things like clocks ticking and newly ironed dresses and hot baths, she asks, "Do any human beings ever realize life while they live it?—every, every minute?"[3] We know the answer: no.

No, we do not realize life while we live it, and we do not look at each other, and we miss too many opportunities to be present with one another. We have to remind ourselves over and over to give the gift of simple attention to life and to those we love.

There is a poem for the Christmas season that I read every year. It is a poignant reminder of how precious our time with one another is. Even in our families, we are "host" and "guest," sharing moments that will never be repeated and may, indeed, be some of the last we have with one another. Titled "Touch Hands," it is by William Henry Harrison Murray:

Ah friends, dear friends,
as years go on and heads get
gray, how fast the guests do go!

Touch hands, touch hands,
With those that stay.

Strong hands to weak,
old hands to young,
around the Christmas board,
touch hands.

The false forget, the foe
forgive, for every guest will
go and every fire burn low
and cabin empty stand.

Forget, forgive, for who may
say that Christmas day may never
come to host or guest again.
Touch hands![4]

The gift of hospitality is a gift of self, a gift of trust, a gift of courage. As host and guest share a mutual exchange of presence, it is a holy gift of the Spirit in their midst. Even if host or guest is not aware of the sacred aspect of their exchange, it exists nevertheless. The holy intimacy of strangers is, after all, the conversation with the Spirit that transpires inside us as much as in our external interactions. I think that is what happened for my friend Misty on a snowy morning in New York.

When Misty, a long-time resident of Manhattan, witnessed people jumping to their deaths from the towers of the World Trade Center on September 11, 2001, the images stirred a memory from many years before. Like the world's overwhelming response of empathy in the wake of that tragedy, her experience of long ago speaks to me of the deepest of bonds between strangers—a bond of caring for the pain of a stranger and of wanting to hold that person's spirit with a sense of dignity and respect. Misty writes:

> There is nothing quite like a snowy weekend day in Manhattan. We are so inured to the throbbing sound of the city that its sudden, soft absence is oddly heart breaking. One Friday night as the snow began, I eagerly looked out my window and set the clock for very early morning on Saturday. I rose, opened a window and listened hungrily for the stillness, then threw on some clothes and boots and headed out to find a "comfort food" breakfast. I walked across West End Avenue toward Broadway

and my favorite coffee shop. To my left was the open courtyard of one of those upper West Side buildings that are appropriately always named the something "Arms."

Almost directly in the center of the courtyard was the prone body of a woman. She was dressed in hat, coat, and gloves, and her purse was over her arm. It was obvious that she was dead and that she had jumped only moments earlier from a window in the building above. The snow was still falling, and there was the slightest dusting over her body. The city was quiet—deathly quiet. There was no one about but the two of us. I did not want somehow to disturb her just yet. There was no question of saving her life. That was over. I approached and stood next to her for a time—our time. I am not given to formal prayer, but am very much a person of reflection. I felt that she should have some time in quietude to finish the journey she had begun when she stepped from the windowsill very much as someone else would step out the door to run mundane errands. I suppose I wanted her soul to have a moment to linger, watch and then move on before the sirens and bustle began.

And so we were together for a time. I wondered if [had some other stranger been a listener the night before] she would have jumped at all. I grieved for the lonely desperation that had taken possession of her life force. I grieved that the ambivalence of the city had betrayed her in her time of need, that she had not found the stranger/friend who could persuade her to get beyond this moment's crisis in hopes that life could open doors for her again. I stayed with her until I felt her time was over, and then I touched her cold arm and left to walk to Broadway where I flagged down the first police car I saw.

BEYOND PITY TO COMPASSION

It stands to reason that if shutting out our own pain makes us callous to the pain of others,[5] letting it in makes us more compassionate. But that is not enough. Misty responded to the strange woman's pain, wanting to make space for the completion of her journey, but she also acted from her respect for the beauty and integrity of another human soul. If all we can see is the pain—in ourselves and in others—we may never be able to see beyond the goal of relieving the pain. Relieving suffering is a worthy objective, but that is not the fullness of compassion, for to focus only on the pain—whether it is our own or another person's—is to inspire more pity than compassion. A friend told me recently that she did not want people in her church to know she was experiencing difficulty in her life because she did not want their pity. I do not blame her. Pity is more offensive than indifference. Pity, however, is as far as we can get if we do not see the beauty in another human being.

Just as we need to know our own pain to respond to the suffering of another, so also we have to see the beauty in ourselves to see the beauty in another. The importance of this aspect of compassion comes across in a story that Alice Walker relates. When she was a young child, she enjoyed being smart and pretty. Then one day when she was eight years old, her brother shot her in the eye with a BB gun, and he and another brother insisted that she not betray the source of her injury. Although she was blinded in that eye, she was most upset about the blemish to her face. The cute little girl was afraid to be seen; she looked down as other children stared or asked about her eye, which was distinguished by a hideous glob of white scar tissue. The smart little girl began doing poorly in school. She hated the eye and cursed its ugly blemish on her life. She did not pray for sight; she prayed for beauty.

A surgical procedure on her eye when she was fourteen removed the white blob, but left a bluish crater in its place. With this dramatic improvement in her appearance, Alice raised her head and graduated valedictorian of her class. But she continued to feel self-conscious of her blind eye.

Then, one day when she was twenty-seven, she was putting her daughter to bed. Rebecca was almost three; she watched a television program called "Big Blue Marble" every day. On this evening, suddenly she focused on her mother's eye. Alice cringed, preparing to protect herself from a child's cruel honesty. Instead, Rebecca studied the eye, even holding her mother's face in her dimpled little hands. Then she said, "Mommy, there's a world in your eye."

"For the most part," writes Walker, "the pain left then. . . . Yes indeed, I realized, looking into the mirror. There *was* a world in my eye. And I saw that it was possible to love it: that in fact, for all it had taught me of shame and anger and inner vision, I *did* love it."[6]

There was a world in her eye, a world of pain *and* of beauty. When Walker was able to see beyond her own pain and affirm the world in her eye, she was freed from anger and shame into compassion, beginning with compassion for herself.

Before we can respond to the pain in the world, we must know our own pain.

Before we can see the beauty in the world and affirm it, we must know our own beauty.

Pity may inspire us to want to do something to relieve suffering, but compassion does more. Compassion affirms others in such a way that they are able to affirm themselves. If they, in turn, see a world of pain and beauty in the eye of their neighbor, they, too, become the source of hope for a more loving human community.

"Do you want anything on your hot dog?" the server asked the child, after his mother said *"No hot dog."*

"Ketchup!"

"Coming up!"

"Mom," said the child, *"she thinks I'm real."*

Observing this scene, David Rankin wrote, "the odor of thick and greasy food permeated the room—but his was a hunger beyond all power to suppress."[7]

No matter what our age or circumstances, there is a world in our eyes and a hunger in our hearts for the kind of presence that is the expression of hospitality. We all need to know that someone thinks we are real.

CHAPTER NINE

SOMETHING THERE IS THAT DOESN'T LOVE A WALL

IN NOVEMBER 1989, THE BERLIN WALL, SYMBOL OF THE Cold War, began to tumble, as the Communist barricade gave way to allow free passage between East and West Berlin. In late December of that year, the Brandenburg Gate section of the wall was opened. About that time, my husband and I went to Germany to visit with family who were stationed at Hahn Air Force Base. After our holiday visit, we planned to go to Berlin for New Year's Eve and get ourselves a chunk of the wall. The traffic, however, was dreadful, and it was clear we would not make it to Berlin before year's end, so we stopped in Frankfurt and checked into the Marriott Hotel. In Germany, people celebrate the New Year with fireworks everywhere. Knowing this, we decided to go to the Marriott party, which included a 360 degree view from the top of the hotel of the fireworks all over the city.

Of course, we didn't know anyone at the party; in fact, we were not aware of other Americans attending. Most of our fellow revelers were German or Japanese. Our ability to converse in German was pretty minimal, so we did a lot of smiling and nodding and pointing as we shared our enthusiasm for the spectacle of colorful explosions bursting all around us.

Just before midnight, as if a magnet were pulling us all away from the windows to a more compelling scene, we were drawn to a corner of the room where we crowded to watch a live television broadcast from the newly opened Brandenburg Gate. Then, as we lifted our glasses to toast a new year and a new decade, we looked directly at one another—Americans, Germans, and Japanese—and our toast held also our common bond of witness to the dismantling of a wall of fear and death. There, where fireworks exploded over a city that had been rebuilt after the devastating bombing of World War II, we felt ourselves held in an incredible moment of grace and ecstasy—a moment full of possibility, openness, and goodwill. It was a moment of history and of healing, of past horror and future hope.

We did not make it to Berlin to get a remnant of the wall, but we did bring back an invisible piece of it in our hearts.

"Something there is that doesn't love a wall," wrote Robert Frost in his poem "Mending Wall." Yes, it was that something inside and among us that felt touched by the Spirit that night. We would not all have described our experience in spiritual terms, but I believe there was a sacred dimension to the bond that transcended language and invited us into a place of forgiveness, reconciliation, and vision. Anthropologist Victor Turner describes this kind of experience as *communitas*. *Communitas* is what happens when a whole group of people cross a threshold together and enter an in-between time that is neither past nor present, and a space that is neither here nor there. In that liminal or threshold space, they receive a glimpse of the possibility that exists among them. Barriers that separate them, such as racial or cultural differences, religious perspectives, or economic status, become irrelevant. In *communitas,* people experience a comradeship in and out of time that reveals, however fleetingly, some recognition of a larger social bond. Everyone is equal. Everyone *feels* what it is to be equal, and their experience gives them hope for who we can be as a human family.[1]

Most experiences of *communitas* occur in extraordinary circumstances, such as our New Year's Eve toast in Germany. They inspire people to create a similar experience in the community where they live—to construct a utopian system where cultures do not clash and all people are truly equal.

Occasionally people can sustain the vision. More often, the feeling of solidarity gives way to the pressures of human division. It is as if we are programmed to create walls of prejudice or power or greed, even though we know as sure as we have ever known anything that we are brothers and sisters bound by a vision of harmony that sustains us and draws us forward.

HINTS OF HOLINESS

Here and there, however, we may encounter a community where people have been able to sustain something of the quality of relationship that is intimated in the experience of *communitas*. For example, my friend Lee Barker visited an island in Indonesia. There, in spite of ongoing religious strife that plagued other parts of the country, he experienced an extraordinary unity among people of diverse religions. Lombok is a remote and undeveloped island, which, like nearly all of Southeast Asia, is shaped by religious influences. Centuries ago, Lombok was settled by the Sasak people from Northwest India and Burma. The people who inhabit the island now are mostly Muslim, but there still remain some who practice the animist religion of those early settlers, the Sasaks. There are also some Hindus who live and worship there. The people are isolated from our century, and perhaps from others in their nation, and they are poor. An older world echoes throughout. Of his experience there, Lee wrote:

> My wife and I hired a driver and a guide to tour the island. As we planned our itinerary, our guide said, "You must see the temple called Pura Lingsar. It has the holly L's." "The what?" we asked. We hadn't picked it up. "The holly L's," he answered. "Oh

all right," we agreed, although we still had no idea what he was talking about.

Pura Lingsar, a temple for worshippers of all three faiths of Lombok, was one of the most wondrous human creations either of us had ever seen. For more than 275 years, whole families of Hindus, Sasaks, and Muslims have made their pilgrimage to the temple where they all worship and where, for some time at least, they all live together. That's right. In the courtyard of the temple, whole families of people of different faiths live for up to a week at a time; cooking, worshipping, sleeping, washing, all together as if they are the closest of kin. And of course, one and all, they love "the holly L's."

The holly L's? That was our guide's pronunciation for "the holy eels." On the premises, there is a pool where eels live behind its lip. They are coaxed out, into sight, by hard boiled eggs that they cannot resist. I never was able to discern why the people of Lombok called the eels holy, but I believe they were. For crowded around them, arm and arm, wide with smiles, were people of all faiths, worshipping together as if there were no boundaries between them. Holy, indeed.

Yes, holy, indeed. It is to these supposedly "primitive" people, perhaps, that we need to look for a model of unity, particularly between people of different religious and cultural traditions. On an island in Southeast Asia, strangers live among one another as if they existed in a mythic time and space set apart from the supposedly civilized world. It is they, however, who demonstrate a more civilized way of being, offering us a gift from the past that endures in the present and creates hope for the future.

SIGNS OF SOLIDARITY

In the months following the September 11, 2001, terrorist attacks on the United States, perceptions and misconceptions about the Islamic religion took center stage in the media. Although in the United States there was an outbreak of bigotry in attacks against Muslims, Sikhs, and people who appeared to be Arab, there were also widely circulated news items or commentaries educating the public with regard to Islamic beliefs; American Muslim leaders denounced the acts of terrorism that had been done in the name of their religion. Story after story circulated, affirming a new sensitivity people felt toward their neighbors. At the same time, many American Muslims feared leaving their own homes. A diverse people with a tradition of welcoming the stranger, we Americans also looked upon one another with suspicion. Our emergent sense of community and solidarity was besmirched with the lingering shadow of xenophobia.

Recalling the shameful internment of Japanese-Americans that occurred after the Japanese attacked Pearl Harbor, however, Americans seemed more conscious of the dangers of rounding up people on the basis of their race or ethnicity as if they were in conspiracy with the enemy. No, we were not so noble as to have achieved a unity among people of diverse cultures or religions, but we seemed to have progressed toward the ideal and felt a sense of pride and solidarity in extending a hand of friendship and understanding to our Islamic neighbors. In cities such as mine, hundreds of people crowded together in unprecedented interfaith gatherings, seeking a common language of faith for their expressions of sorrow, their prayers of healing, and their songs of hope.

The pain of this wound on America was also felt throughout the world. Many of the victims of the attacks were, in fact, from other lands. We entered a liminal time—a time when we knew immediately that life as we have known it was over. People all over the world knew it too, and the outpouring of grief and solidarity was overwhelming. I was moved to tears when I went to an Internet site that was nothing but photographs of people in other countries, mostly at American embassies or consulates, lighting candles, praying, or offering flowers. Most moving to me were the demonstrations of solidarity in Tokyo and in several Russian and German cities: Moscow, St. Petersburg, Frankfurt, Hamburg, Munich. Flags were at half-mast at the Kremlin, and a ribbon in Berlin read "God Bless the World." These nations, once our despised enemies, now joined with us in expression of solidarity.

One of the most stirring accounts of international community was related by an officer who sent an e-mail from aboard the guided missile destroyer *USS Winston S. Churchill* shortly after the September 11 attacks. While they had been in port, members of the *Churchill* crew had gotten together with crew members from the German destroyer, the *GFS Lutjens* (D-185) for a sports day and cookout. Now back at sea, they got a call from *Lutjens* requesting permission to pass close by their port side, to say good-bye. The American crew prepared to render them honors on the bridge wing. As *Lutjens* made its approach, it was announced that the German warship was flying an American flag. Then, as they came closer, they could see that it was flying at half-mast. The officer described what happened next:

> [*Lutjens*] came up along side and we saw that the entire crew of the German ship were manning the rails, in their dress blues. They had made up a sign that was displayed on the side that read "We Stand by You." Needless to say there was not a dry eye on the bridge as they stayed alongside us for a few minutes and we cut our salutes. It was probably the most powerful thing I have seen in my entire life and more than a few of us fought to retain our composure. . . . The German Navy did an incredible thing for this crew. . . . It's amazing to think that only a half-century ago things were quite different, and to see the unity that is being demonstrated throughout Europe and the world makes us all feel proud to be out here doing our job.[2]

When I viewed the photograph of the crew of the *Lutjens* showing their support (posted on the U.S. Navy Website with the letter), I too was moved to tears.

WHEN THINGS FALL APART

This story of solidarity is but one among many that circulated in the weeks following the attacks. Shaken by the horror of this attack and its implications for our future, we were reminded of how precious our connections are, not only with fellow Americans but also with fellow citizens of the global village. We were stripped of our normal lines of separation from others and reminded of our vulnerability. Something about that feeling of vulnerability forged a bond of compassion and solidarity among our neighbors in other nations, and out of this tragic and devastating event we were able to see ourselves through the eyes of the world. This was difficult for us, for we saw hatred and resentment as well as empathy, but it was a dose of humility that helped to mature us as a nation among other nations. Particularly with the toppling of the twin towers of international trade and finance and the lingering cloud of death that blackened the skies of daily air travel, many aspects of the consumer economy that supports our lifestyle of comfort and privilege were suddenly subject to greater reflection and introspection.

In her book, *When Things Fall Apart*, Buddhist teacher Pema Chödrön offers wisdom for situations where our structure of meaning is shattered. Affirming the potential for growth in such times, she writes:

> When things fall apart and we're on the verge of we know not what, the test for each of us is to stay on that brink. . . . The very first noble truth of the Buddha points out that suffering is inevitable for human beings as long as we believe that things last—that they don't disintegrate, that they can be counted on to satisfy our hunger for security. From this point of view, the only time we ever know what's really going on is when the rug's been pulled out and we can't find anywhere to land. . . . To stay with

that shakiness—to stay with a broken heart, a rumbling stomach, with the feeling of hopelessness and wanting to get revenge— that is the path of true awakening.[3]

What Chödrön suggests goes against our every instinct. Why would we want to stay with the shakiness? If the rug has been pulled out from underneath us, our impulse is to steady ourselves and find firm footing.

But she is right. It is there in the shakiness, there in uncertainty, that we are both most vulnerable and most receptive to the voice of the Spirit. Like a lobster that has shed its shell, we have the opportunity to grow our soul before we reconstruct our protective shield. This is when we allow ourselves to be touched by a holy vision of unity with all people, particularly those we may call our enemies.

GOD BLESS THE WORLD!

In this shaky in-between space, then, we see possibilities for human community—for a vision of genuine solidarity. The temptation in a time of crisis is to create solidarity among "our own" people, to pursue the impulse to strike back at our attackers, to feel the power of our unity as we pursue the enemy. If we respond out of fear and a demand for justice, however, our urge is to create walls, not tear them down.

As the United States responded to terrorist attacks in 2001, American flags were ubiquitous, and phrases and slogans declared our solidarity as our leaders retaliated against those in Afghanistan who harbored Osama bin Laden and other Islamic radicals who had orchestrated the terrorist attacks. Prevalent among the slogans were "God bless America," "United we stand," and "In God we trust." Although I had no particular aversion to either flags or an invocation of divine blessing, I became concerned that this kind of response was more like a pep rally for a football game than it was a genuine expression of patriotism. Also, in a nation of many faiths, it is important that we not use the name of God as if we have a special corner on the Absolute. A notion of nationalistic unity is too small for God, and our trust is suspicious if we do not experience trust in God through our bond of trust with our human companions throughout the world. The solidarity that derives from divine power draws us toward peace, not war. The patriotism that operates out of trust in God exhibits an international, interfaith perspective, not nationalistic fervor.

As we move through a time of recovery and self-assessment, we also have the opportunity to examine our sense of spiritual strength and act according to commonly held spiritual values. Can we cultivate a new kind of pride? America is a powerful nation. Yes, we have been blessed, and we have the opportunity to use our power and prosperity to bless the world. It is in our generosity and our hospitality, not our military might, that we fulfill the promise of our founders. A substantial military industrial complex has rendered us powerful, to be sure, but we have a responsibility to use our power in the service of justice and human community.

Strangely enough, one positive outcome of the terrorist attacks is that more Americans have awakened to seeing themselves through the eyes of the rest of the world, most of whom do not earn as much in a year as an average American family spends on dinner at a restaurant. We do not condone monstrous acts of mass murder, but in our effort to understand why our nation is the object of such passionate and zealous hatred we have had to hear the accusations. We cannot deny that we generate much of the world's pollution and are the largest contributor to global warming. We allow our corporations to exploit labor of all ages in other countries, and we support despotic and cruel regimes to ensure the flow of resources to us. As we identify some of our own complicity in generating ill will, we take a bitter dose of humility, but it is ultimately to our benefit.

The Reverend Daniel W. Murphy is a Roman Catholic priest whose younger brother died in the 2001 World Trade Center attack. These words he spoke the following Sunday hold up a vision of the kind of patriotism and pride that I am talking about:

> Yes, we need to act to end terrorism. But we cannot allow our hearts to be filled with hatred, anger, and revenge. History teaches us that revenge builds upon revenge and more revenge. It never ends. Yes, we need to seek justice. But we need to seek a justice based not on hatred or anger over what has happened, but rather out of concern for the future of all the human community. . . .
>
> When I see all these flags everyone is waving or wearing, I hope and I pray they are symbols of our solidarity, our union as a nation, in grieving and in reaching out in love and compassion to those who have suffered loss. . . .

If you have an American flag outside your house, if you wear an American flag, wear it and display it with pride. But not pride in guns, not pride in bombs or high-tech weapons of revenge. Let it be a source of pride that we can be a people who respond with love, compassion, and healing to end the evil, not only in the terrorists, but the evil and the darkness that exists in every one of us, male and female, young and old. Let it be a symbol of pride that we are a people who have always welcomed the stranger and not shut out those who are different from ourselves.[4]

IMAGINE!

In the midst of World War II, no one could have imagined that American, Japanese, and German citizens would be toasting a new year together, celebrating also the destruction of the Berlin Wall. In the midst of the cold war, no one could have imagined that the people of the former Soviet Union would congregate at American embassies or lower their flag to half-mast at the Kremlin in a show of solidarity with the United States.

As I write this chapter in 2001, I cannot really imagine reconciliation with those who murdered thousands of innocent people on September 11. I am inspired toward the vision, however, by the words of Father Murphy and by the witness of people of faith who have testified to the power of love over fear and hatred. Daphne B. Noyes, for example, an Episcopal deacon, was on duty as a chaplain at Ground Zero on the eve of Thanksgiving, standing at the pit where relief workers toiled night and day recovering the remains of victims of the World Trade Center attack. The bodies of two firefighters were discovered, but it took hours to release them from the rubble of the tower that had become a tomb. Finally, around 2:00 A.M., the remains were liberated, shrouded, and ready for the ritual salute and prayers. Noyes stood among the ruins, flanked by firemen, the two flag-draped bodies at her feet. Reflecting on this moment, she wrote, "As I led the men in the Lord's Prayer, I wondered what it was like for them to stand in the very place where so many had lost so much and utter the words, 'Forgive us our trespasses as we forgive those who trespass against us.' . . . In the pit, as in our hearts, we clamber on the steep and rocky incline to reach the very center where our hopes and fears lie tangled in the wreckage of this fallen, beautiful world. We are challenged as much to remember our trespasses as we are to forgive those who trespass against us."[5]

Among the survivors of the attack on the World Trade Center was a young man named Usman Farman, a Pakistani Muslim who worked on the south side of Building Seven. Only two days after the tragic events of September 11, Farman spoke at a ceremony at Bentley College, where he had graduated the previous May. He described an encounter with a stranger that proliferated into cyberspace as an image of hope, not just for recovery from this event but for peace and reconciliation among people who have been held in the grip of conflict for decades. This is his description of what happened after he evacuated the building:

With a thousand people staring, we [watched] in shock as the first tower collapsed. . . . The next thing I remember is that a dark cloud of glass and debris about fifty stories high came tumbling towards us. I turned around and ran as fast as possible, [and] fell down trying to get away. What happened next is why I came here to give this speech.

I was on my back, facing this massive cloud that was approaching. It must have been six hundred feet off; everything was already dark. I normally wear a pendant around my neck, inscribed with an Arabic prayer for safety. A Hasidic Jewish man came up to me and held the pendant in his hand and looked at it. He read the Arabic out loud for a second. What he said next, I will never forget. With a deep Brooklyn accent he said, "Brother, if you don't mind, there is a cloud of glass coming at us, grab my hand, let's get the hell out of here." He helped me stand up, and we ran for what seemed like forever without looking back. He was the last person I would ever have thought would help me. If it weren't for him, I probably would have been engulfed in shattered glass and debris.[6]

Farman's story takes on mythic dimensions, holding up the image of a Jew reaching across traditional lines of enmity to offer help to a Muslim, and inviting us to recognize that we are not so very different from our strange or estranged neighbors, for we belong to one human family, all equal in the eyes of God, Allah, the Holy. We recognize, in these moments when we open our shut-up hearts to one another, that we are, as Charles Dickens phrased it, "fellow passengers to the grave."

Oh, how we do long in the depth of our souls to feel our bond with others as we intuit what it was meant to be from the beginning of time. If there is a grand design for the universe, it is in the image of these hands clasped in a moment that is as timeless and cosmic as it is particular to its place in the history of the world. It says love each other, regardless, and forgive those who trespass against you just as you need forgiveness for your transgressions and shortcomings.

Our experience of solidarity, then, generates a power in the world— a power we do not really understand, for it is a holy power not ours to give or use. It is, rather, a power and grace in which we participate. It embraces us, binds us together, and heals us, even though it is not ours to claim.

LED TO PLACES WE DID NOT PLAN TO GO

Having a vision of harmony and love is one thing; implementing it is another. Something there is that doesn't love a wall, but something there is also that *does* love a wall. We build walls so we can define who is right and who is wrong or who is good and who is evil, making sure we are on the side of what is good and right. Walls help us create the illusion that our hostile feelings are justified by being on the right side.

Walls also perpetuate our fears and protect us from facing them. Bringing these inner walls down is the spiritual task that challenges us as individuals and as communities with the power of our joined vision. Whether we are addressing the wounds of a close familial rift or working toward world peace, it is essential that we keep before us a vision of what is possible when we call upon the power of the Spirit.

Asking for divine guidance, however, is not something we can do casually. We are inclined, particularly when things fall apart, to pray for guidance and invoke spiritual presence. But I am reminded of the words of my friend and mentor, Sharon Daloz Parks, who posed the question, "How do we know when God is with us?" Then she answered, "We know because we will be led to places we did not plan to go."[7] In these words, Sharon offers another version of the familiar caveat, "Be careful what you pray for; you might get it." To pray for God's presence or guidance might mean having to change your way of thinking and behaving.

Annie Dillard reinforces Sharon's notion of what it means to invoke divine power:

> Does anyone have the foggiest idea what sort of power we so blithely invoke? Or, as I suspect, does no one believe a word of it? The churches are children playing on the floor with their chemistry sets, mixing up a batch of TNT to kill a Sunday morning. It is madness to wear ladies' straw hats and velvet hats to church; we should all be wearing crash helmets. Ushers should issue life preservers and signal flares; they should lash us to our pews. For the sleeping god may wake someday and take offense, or the waking god may draw us out to where we can never return.[8]

The fact is, God is not only likely to lead us to places we did not plan to go; it will probably turn out that we don't really want to go there. Chances are, we will be asked to take some risks, open our hearts, or make some personal sacrifice on behalf of the greater good.

RECONCILIATION:
AN EXTRAORDINARY KIND OF LOVE

I heard a story a few years ago that demonstrates what can happen when we don our crash helmets and invite God into our midst. A whole church was led to a place they did not plan to go, to a place where they were asked to move beyond hate and fear and to love their enemy.

They were members of an Episcopal church in San Diego that was burned in the mid-1980s. The arsonist was caught. Members of the congregation, angry and devastated by the loss, wanted him to pay, and they were pleased when he was convicted and sentenced to serve a term in prison.

After the fire, they held services in the Parish Hall. In their grief and fatigue, they took the first steps toward recovery. Although they had been devastated by the fire, and did not have clergy leadership during the aftermath, they held church suppers, plays and concerts, and they conducted a capital campaign. They called the Rev. Susan Tobias as their new rector, and with a boost of energy and spirit from her leadership, they were well on their way to completing their building fund and accepting the design for the new building when they heard the news: the arsonist was up for parole.

The old feelings resurfaced—anger, hurt . . . and the fear that he would strike again. Susan had not been there through the fire and its aftermath; she wondered who this man was and why he had set fire to the building. She decided to write to him and ask if she could visit him in prison.

The arsonist, Henry, told her a therapy group had helped him. At the time he had set the fire, he was angry and confused. He had not chosen the church; it was just there at the wrong time.

Over the next month, Susan visited Henry again and told the congregation about the visits. They were shocked, but how could they tell their priest not to visit "those in prison"? She continued to see him, preparing him for his release. He wrote a letter to the parish saying that he was sorry for burning the church, and she published it in the parish newsletter.

She spoke to the congregation of the need to place a new event in their history that would surpass the arson in meaning. When his parole came up, Susan helped Henry get on disability, find a board and care home, and shop for food and cigarettes. After two years, he was in a stable housing situation, taking medication for mental illness, and attending local AA meetings. Members of the congregation helped him find work or gathered furniture and kitchenware for his apartment. Several people tutored him so he could take the graduate equivalency exam for a high school diploma.

During his parole, Henry was subject to a restraining order forbidding him to come near the church grounds, but when he was released from his parole, he attended a service in the new building, and at announcement time, he came forward. With simplicity and honesty, he apologized for burning the church and thanked the congregation for their forgiveness. He called them his community. Although Susan has since moved away to another parish, members of the congregation have continued to make a place for this troubled young man.

WALKING THE ROAD OF HOPE

When tragedy strikes, when evil shows its ugly face in the hearts of good people, when fear and compassion vie for your soul or mine, what gives us hope?

Not blame. Not even justice. Punish the criminal, but that does not give us hope. Blame, justice, and revenge are a way to cope—to grope or grasp for security and some kind of satisfaction that never comes.

The power of hope, however, resides in the human heart, in a vulnerable and generous place where there is not judgment; in a place where, even though there is recognition of good and evil, there is not a distinction between good people and bad people, between us and them.

Whoever is without sin should throw the first stone, said Jesus, when a crowd was poised to stone a woman caught in adultery. No stones were thrown. Bible scholar Robert Funk has suggested starting the "First Stone Club." Give each person a stone, he says, and see how long we can hold on to them.

Throwing stones is easy, especially when people do very bad things. Keeping a good, safe distance from known criminals is understandable, especially when they have violated us.

The power of hope resides in a place in the human heart where we are not safe, and our path is not easy. It is the most natural, logical thing in the world to put up walls between us the good people and them the bad people; but the Spirit has a logic all its own. Don't expect it to make sense. It won't. Punishment, retribution, revenge, retaliation: these make sense when laws natural or human are violated. Forgiveness and loving the enemy: these only make sense in the Spirit's domain. No, this logic does not fit with our usual schemes of justice, and it is not even the path our world asks us to take. It is instead the path our souls long to create.

A Chinese philosopher once asked if we could even say there is such a thing as hope in the world. Then he said, "Hope is like a road in the country; there was never a road, but when many people walk on it, the road comes into existence."[9]

NOTES

INTRODUCTION

   1. Lindbergh, A. M. *Gift from the Sea.* New York: Vintage, 1965, pp. 118–119.

   2. I want to offer a few words here about what I mean when I speak of Spirit or the Spirit. *Spirit* is the word I use to name the unnamable. My personal faith tradition is Unitarian Universalist. As a Unitarian who conceives multiplicity in unity, I experience Spirit as the divine presence within me, around me, and beyond my human experience. As a Universalist who has affinity with Christian, Buddhist, Jewish, and Taoist traditions (and a persistent and romantic streak of pantheism), I relate to Spirit in the particular stories, myths, and teachings of many faiths, walking paths where others have walked and exploring scriptures engraved in human memory. Spirit is the holy allurement that draws me into its numinous presence, where I know I *belong* in some cosmic and eternal way. It is immanent and transcendent, material and illusory. I call its presence into my soul, and it calls me (sometimes kicking and screaming) into its Soul. The gadfly of grace, the vital essence of virtue, the Spirit is my source of sustenance, strength, and transformation; it infuses life with joy and humor. It is the creative energy and connective tissue that grounds and uplifts me—my source of hope,

compassion, and vision as I seek to make a difference during my short stay on planet Earth. Spirit speaks to me in the grandeur of Himalayan peaks and the mournful eyes of a hungry child. Sometimes I relate to God as Spirit, but when I do, I am not thinking of a father in heaven looking down on his creation; for me God is father and mother at the same time that God has no gender at all. God is not a person, but God as Spirit calls me into the most personal of relationships with God's self.

3. From a sermon by Marilyn Sewell, preached Jan. 3, 1999, at the First Unitarian Church, Portland, Oregon.

CHAPTER ONE   MOMENT OF TRUTH

1. Lindbergh (1965), p. 23.

2. For those discussions, I used material from Simon, S. B., Howe, L. W., and Kirschenbaum, H. *Values Clarification: A Handbook of Practical Strategies for Teachers and Students.* Hart, New York: 1972.

3. Frankl, V. *Man's Search for Meaning: An Introduction to Logotherapy.* New York: Washington Square Press, 1959, 1963, pp. 104–106.

CHAPTER TWO   BONDS OF FREEDOM

1. benShea, N. *Jacob the Baker: Gentle Wisdom for a Complicated World.* New York: Ballantine, 1989, pp. 95–96.

2. Fromm, E. *The Art of Loving.* New York: HarperCollins, 1956, p. 28.

3. Fromm (1956), pp. 40–41.

4. Angelou, M. *Wouldn't Take Nothing for My Journey Now.* New York: Random House, 1993, p. 129.

5. Excerpted from Stephen, C. S., Jr. (ed.). *The Gift of the Ordinary.* Boston: Unitarian Universalist Association, 1985, p. 14.

6. Palmer, P. *The Company of Strangers: Christians and the Renewal of America's Public Life.* New York: Crossroad, 1981, p. 67.

7. Palmer (1981), pp. 67–69.

CHAPTER THREE   CLOSE TO HOME

1. Putnam, R. D. *Bowling Alone: The Collapse and Revival of American Community.* New York: Simon & Schuster, 2000, p. 147.

2. Putnam (2000), p. 19.

3. Steve Martin, from the Mediation Center of Asheville, North Carolina, provided this example.

4. Berry, W. *The Unsettling of America: Culture and Agriculture.* New York: Avon, 1977, pp. 28–29.

CHAPTER FOUR   FEAR ITSELF

1. Putnam (2000), p. 136.

2. Bartlett, J. *Bartlett's Familiar Quotations.* (E. Morison Beck, ed.) New York: Little, Brown, 1980, p. 381.

3. Bartlett (1980), p. 813.

4. Roosevelt, F. D. *The Wit and Wisdom of Franklin D. Roosevelt.* (M. Meyersohn, ed.) Boston: Beacon Press, 1950, pp. 10–11.

5. Bartlett (1980), p. 557.

6. Proverbs 3:25, Revised Standard Version.

7. Herbert, B. "Living with Fear." *New York Times,* Oct. 15, 2001.

8. Grossman, D. "Beastly Life Under the Thumb of Terror." *Los Angeles Times,* July 29, 1996.

9. The classic story of Jacob's encounter with God is told in Genesis 32:22–32, Revised Standard Version.

CHAPTER FIVE   THERE BUT FOR THE GRACE OF GOD . . .

1. Crossan, J. D. *The Essential Jesus: What Jesus Really Taught.* San Francisco: HarperSanFrancisco, 1994, p. 60.

2. Crossan (1994), p. 49.

CHAPTER SIX   SECRETS AND STRANGERS

1. Hawthorne, N. "The Ambitious Guest." In *Introduction to the Short Story* (C. E. Redman, ed.). Cincinnati, Ohio: McCormick-Mathers, 1965, pp. 87–96.

2. Coleridge, S. T. "The Rime of the Ancient Mariner." In R. Wilbur and R. Strange (eds.), *Coleridge.* New York: Dell, 1959, pp. 41–61.

3. Tillich, P. *The Courage to Be.* New Haven: Yale University Press, 1952, pp. 164–165.

CHAPTER SEVEN   SHADOWS AND STRANGERS

1. Putnam (2000), pp. 176–177.

2. Blake, W. *The Portable Blake.* New York: Viking, 1946, pp. 114–115.

3. Tavris, C. *Anger: The Misunderstood Emotion.* New York: Simon & Schuster, 1982, p. 226.

4. Although a couples group in our church would now include same-sex couples, it was, at that time, a group of married men and women.

5. Golding, W. *Lord of the Flies.* New York: Perigree, 1954, p. 143.

6. Twain, M. "The Damned Human Race." In B. DeVoto (ed.), *Letters from the Earth: The Uncensored Writings by Mark Twain.* New York: HarperPerennial, 1962, pp. 225–226.

7. Frank, A. *The Diary of a Young Girl: The Definitive Edition.* (O. H. Frank and M. Pressler, eds.) New York: Doubleday, 1991, p. 332.

CHAPTER EIGHT   HOSPITALITY: THE GIFT OF PRESENCE

1. Rankin, D. *Portraits from the Cross.* Boston: Unitarian Universalist Association, 1978, p. 34.

2. Palmer (1981), p. 69.

3. Wilder, T. *Our Town.* New York: Avon, 1957, p. 138.

4. In Seaburg, C. (ed.). *Celebrating Christmas: An Anthology.* Boston: Unitarian Universalist Ministers Association, 1983, p. 70.

5. See discussion of the shadow in Chapter Seven.

6. Walker, A. *In Search of Our Mothers' Gardens.* Orlando: Harcourt Brace, 1983, pp. 384–393.

7. Rankin (1978), p. 34.

CHAPTER NINE

SOMETHING THERE IS THAT DOESN'T LOVE A WALL

1. Turner, V. *The Ritual Process: Structure and Antistructure.* Ithaca, N.Y.: Cornell University Press, 1969, p. vii. *Communitas* is discussed in greater depth in Chapter Five of my book, *Pilgrim Heart: The Inner Journey Home.*

2. This story was related, along with photographs of the *Lutjen* crew's demonstration of solidarity, on the U.S. Navy's Website at www.chinfo.navy.mil/navpalib/news/news_stories/pentstruck19.html.

3. Chödrön, P. *When Things Fall Apart: Heart Advice for Difficult Times.* Boston: Shambhala, 1997, pp. 9–10.

4. Murphy, D. W. "Brotherly Love." In F. Church (ed.), *Restoring Faith: America's Religious Leaders Answer Terror with Hope.* New York: Walker, 2001, pp. 48–51.

5. D. Noyes, from a sermon preached at Emmanuel Church in the City of Boston, Dec. 9, 2001.

6. Adapted from an e-mail copy of Farman's speech and used with permission from Usman Farman.

7. Parks, S. "Led to Places We Did Not Plan to Go. . . ." *Cresset* (Valparaiso University), Summer 1996, p. 5.

8. Dillard, A. *Teaching a Stone to Talk: Expeditions and Encounters.* New York: Harper Colophon, 1983, pp. 40–41.

9. From "The Epigrams of Lusin." In L. Yutang (ed.), *The Wisdom of China and India.* New York: Modern Library, 1942, p. 1087.

THE AUTHOR

Sarah York is a Unitarian Universalist minister who has served congregations in New York, Maryland, California, and England. She earned her undergraduate degree from Wake Forest University, and a master's degree from Duke University, and taught high school English for eleven years before she trained for the ministry at Harvard Divinity School. As the author of *Remembering Well: Rituals for Celebrating Life and Mourning Death* (Jossey-Bass, 2000), she conducts workshops on "Rituals of Remembrance for the Seasons of Grief." She is also the author of *Pilgrim Heart: The Inner Journey Home* (Jossey-Bass, 2001) and *Into the Wilderness.* She lives on a farm in the mountains of western North Carolina with her husband, Chuck, where she grows herbs, flowers, and vegetables, and enjoys creating ways to share the harvest with others.